FRONTIERS IN THE SOIL
THE ARCHAEOLOGY OF GEORGIA

By
ROY S. DICKENS, JR.
and
JAMES L. McKINLEY

In Collaboration With

JAMES H. CHAPMAN and LELAND G. FERGUSON

Carl Vinson Institute of Government

Originally published in 1979 by Frontiers Publishing Company

Carl Vinson Institute of Government, University of Georgia, Athens 30602
© 2003 by the Society for Georgia Archaeology
All rights reserved. Published 2003

Printed in Mexico

ISBN 0-89854-208-1

The cover illustration depicts a ceremony during the Mississippian period (A.D. 800 to 1540). Priests are shown dressed as mythical beings. These ceremonies were important in making people aware of the power of their leaders and in communicating with the spirits of nature.

CONTENTS

PREFACE TO THE SECOND PRINTING

THIS ENTERTAINING YET INFORMATIVE BOOK THAT USES ARCHAEOLOGY TO EXPLORE GEORGIA HISTORY AND PREHISTORY WAS CREATED BY GEORGIA ARCHAEOLOGIST ROY DICKENS JR. AND ARTIST JAMES MCKINLEY. INTENDED FOR THE MIDDLE SCHOOL-AGE READER, ITS HAND-LETTERED FONT AND FULL-COLOR DRAWINGS ENGAGE STUDENT AND CASUAL READER ALIKE, AND ITS MESSAGE IS AS TIMELY TODAY AS IT WAS IN 1979. TAKING ADVANTAGE OF THE RICH HISTORIC AND PRE-HISTORIC ARCHAEOLOGICAL HERITAGE OF GEORGIA, THE AUTHORS PROVOKE READERS TO THINK ABOUT VARIATIONS IN CULTURE AND THE INTERACTIONS OF NATIVE AMERICANS AND EARLY EUROPEAN SETTLERS WITH THEIR ENVIRONMENTS OVER LONG PERIODS OF TIME. THE STRONG EDUCATIONAL CONTENT IS ENHANCED BY THE UNDERLYING THEME THAT ARCHAEOLOGICAL SITES ARE ENDANGERED AND THAT THE INFORMATION THEY CONTAIN IS FRAGILE AND IRREPLACEABLE.

MEMBERS OF THE SOCIETY FOR GEORGIA ARCHAEOLOGY (SGA), A NONPROFIT ORGANIZATION CONSISTING OF AVOCATIONAL AND PROFESSIONAL ARCHAEOLOGISTS AND INTERESTED MEMBERS OF THE PUBLIC, RECOGNIZED THE NEED TO BRING BACK INTO PRINT THIS IMPOR-TANT PUBLICATION SO THAT READERS CAN AGAIN BENEFIT FROM IT. SGA MEMBERS ACQUIRED THE COPYRIGHT FOR THIS PUBLICATION AND BEGAN EFFORTS TO FUND ITS REPRINT AND DISTRIBUTION WITH SUPPORT FROM THE OFFICE OF THE STATE ARCHAEOLOGIST IN THE HISTORIC PRESER-VATION DIVISION, GEORGIA DEPARTMENT OF NATURAL RESOURCES. THROUGH A PARTNERSHIP WITH THE CARL VINSON INSTITUTE OF GOVERNMENT, SGA HAS REALIZED THIS GOAL, AND THIS ENGAGING AND CREATIVE BOOK IS AGAIN AVAILABLE. IN ADDITION, THERE IS A SEPAR-ATE TEACHER'S HANDBOOK THAT ALLOWS EDUCATORS TO USE THE BOOK TO TEACH CORE CURRICULUM SCIENCE AND SOCIAL SCIENCE STANDARDS WHILE PRESENTING WAYS IN WHICH TO INVOLVE STUDENTS IN ACTIVITIES WITHOUT ENDANGERING ARCHAEOLOGICAL SITES.

IT IS THE HOPE OF THE MEMBERS OF SGA THAT READERS OF THIS PUBLICATION WILL GAIN AN UNDERSTANDING OF THE IMPORTANCE OF OUR STATE'S ARCHAEOLOGICAL SITES THAT WILL IN TURN FOSTER A SENSE OF RESPECT AND RESPONSIBILITY FOR THIS HERITAGE.

ELIZABETH C. SHIRK, PRESIDENT
THE SOCIETY FOR GEORGIA ARCHAEOLOGY
FEBRUARY 2003

PREFACE TO THE FIRST PRINTING

This book was conceived by archaeologist Roy Dickens and artist James McKinley in 1975, while McKinley was enrolled in Dickens' class at Georgia State University. It took three years for the idea to become a reality. James Chapman, a research associate at Georgia State, contributed many initial ideas and background research. Chapman's death in an automobile accident on April 17, 1977 was an immeasurable loss to the project. Leland Ferguson, archaeologist at the University of South Carolina, provided numerous ideas and constant editorial criticism as the manuscript progressed. He also wrote portions of Chapter I.

Until 1975, McKinley's lifetime interest in archaeology had been totally from an amateur perspective. However, he believed that a study of our state's past had great value for its young people. Dickens, who had been teaching anthropology and archaeology to college students for many years, was also convinced of the need for such a book. He knew it would be especially appropriate for courses in Social Science, Earth Science, and Georgia History.

At first, Dickens was uncertain that McKinley's idea for using cartoon-type illustrations was in keeping with the serious nature of the book's subject matter. But after seeing several sketches, he was convinced that this type of illustration would bring a combination of realism and gentle humor that otherwise would not be possible. Many all-day sessions were required to develop the major themes of the book and to reduce an enormous amount of information to a package that would be manageable for student, teacher, and general reader. The text and illustrations were the work of both authors. However, the finished text was Dickens' responsibility and the finished illustrations McKinley's.

This book became such a "labor of love" for the authors and collaborators, that many colleagues, family members, and friends were easily drawn into the project. Helpful comments were made by Dibbie McKinley, Carol Dickens, Eileen Sellars Roberts, Robert Blakely, Valerie Fennell, Carol Speight, Annette Ferguson, Linda Carnes, Anne Rogers, and David Dickens. Jackie Fishman, Ina Jane Wundram, and David Hally provided final critiques and editing of the manuscript.

THE AUTHORS HOPE THAT READERS OF THIS BOOK WILL NOT USE IT AS A "GUIDE" TO PRACTICE ARCHAEOLOGY. ARCHAEOLOGICAL FIELD WORK SHOULD BE UNDERTAKEN <u>ONLY</u> UNDER THE DIRECT SUPERVISION OF A PROFESSIONAL ARCHAEOLOGIST. EACH ARCHAEOLOGICAL SITE, NO MATTER HOW SMALL, IS LIKE A RARE ONE-OF-A-KIND DOCUMENT. ONCE DAMAGED OR DESTROYED, A SITE CANNOT BE REPLACED. A PRIVATE INDIVIDUAL OR GROUP SIMPLY DOES NOT HAVE THE EXPERIENCE, TRAINING OR FACILITIES TO PROPERLY RECOVER, INTERPRET, AND CARE FOR ARCHAEOLOGICAL REMAINS. OUR AIM IS TO CREATE A SENSE OF RESPONSIBILITY AND RESPECT FOR THE ARCHAEOLOGICAL RESOURCES OF GEORGIA.

ROY S. DICKENS, JR.
AND
JAMES L. McKINLEY

AUGUST, 1978

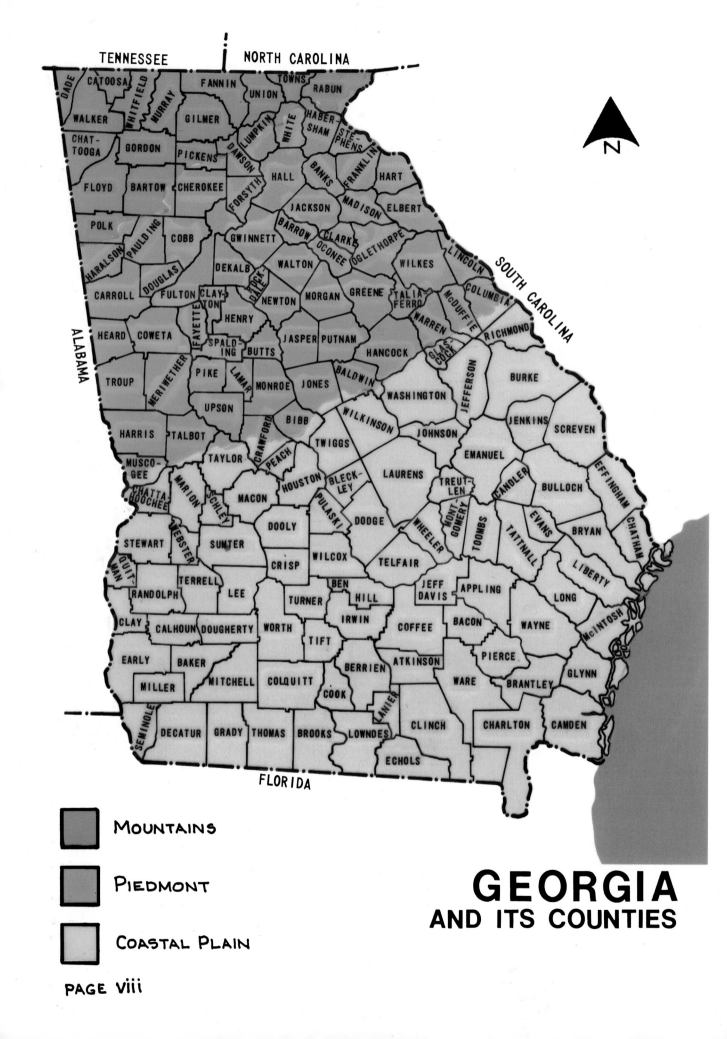

GEORGIA
AND ITS COUNTIES

Mountains

Piedmont

Coastal Plain

PAGE viii

CHAPTER I
WHAT IS ARCHAEOLOGY?

HAVE YOU EVER BEEN WALKING THROUGH THE WOODS, OR A FIELD, OR A VACANT LOT IN THE CITY, AND STOPPED TO PICK UP AN INTERESTING LOOKING OBJECT FROM THE GROUND? PERHAPS THE OBJECT CAUGHT YOUR EYE BECAUSE OF ITS SHAPE, COLOR, OR THE MATERIAL FROM WHICH IT WAS MADE. MAYBE THE OBJECT WAS AN ANCIENT STONE SPEARHEAD, AN OLD BOTTLE NECK, OR SIMPLY A RUSTY NAIL WITH A DIFFERENT SHAPE FROM THE NAILS WE USE TODAY. IF YOU ARE CURIOUS ABOUT OLD OBJECTS SUCH AS THESE, YOU ARE THINKING LIKE AN ARCHAEOLOGIST.

ARCHAEOLOGY IS PART OF THE SOCIAL SCIENCE CALLED <u>ANTHRO-POLOGY.</u> ANTHROPOLOGY IS THE STUDY OF HUMAN GROUPS. ARCHAEOLOGISTS STUDY HUMAN GROUPS THAT HAVE LIVED IN THE PAST— SOMETIMES THOUSANDS OF YEARS AGO—AND THEY OFTEN DIG IN THE SOIL TO FIND CLUES TO HOW THESE GROUPS LIVED.

<u>CULTURAL ANTHROPOLOGISTS</u> STUDY GROUPS OF PEOPLE LIVING TODAY IN VARIOUS PARTS OF THE WORLD. A PEOPLE'S SOCIAL ORGANIZATION, KINSHIP, TECHNOLOGY, ECONOMY, AND LANGUAGE CAN TELL US MUCH ABOUT HOW THEY HAVE ADAPTED TO THEIR ENVIRONMENT. THESE STUDIES CAN ALSO HELP US TO UNDERSTAND HOW OUR OWN SOCIETY HAS DEVELOPED.

<u>PHYSICAL ANTHROPOLOGISTS</u> STUDY THE BIOLOGICAL HERITAGE OF MAN. THEY EXPLORE ANCIENT DEPOSITS IN SEARCH OF FOSSIL HUMAN BONES, AND THEY STUDY THE PHYSICAL CHARACTERISTICS OF GROUPS IN THE MODERN WORLD AS WELL. IF ARCHAEOLOGISTS FIND HUMAN SKELETONS IN THEIR EXCAVATIONS, THEY USUALLY SEND THESE BONES TO A PHYSICAL ANTHROPOLOGIST FOR DETAILED STUDY.

A THIRD GROUP OF ANTHROPOLOGISTS CALL THEMSELVES <u>ARCHAEOLOGISTS.</u> ARCHAEOLOGISTS STUDY THE MATERIAL REMAINS OF PAST HUMAN ACTIVITY. THIS ACTIVITY MAY HAVE TAKEN PLACE SEVERAL MILLION YEARS AGO OR MAYBE ONLY A FEW DOZEN YEARS AGO. ARCHAEOLOGISTS BELIEVE THAT WE WILL NEVER UNDERSTAND PEOPLE OF TODAY WITHOUT STUDYING PEOPLE OF THE PAST.

Sometimes archaeologists find beautiful pieces of art or tombs of great kings, but these are only a small part of the story they are seeking. An archaeologist wants to understand the complete way of life of the people he is studying. For this reason, a burned ear of corn, a broken piece of pottery, or a fragment of a child's toy may be just as important as a beautifully carved statue or a king's tomb.

The soil of Georgia is filled with materials made and discarded by past societies. These things, such as arrowheads, pieces of pottery, and broken bottles are called "artifacts." Each place where artifacts are found is called an archaeological site. Everytime people throw things away, lose things, or disturb the ground in any way, they are making an archaeological site. People have been living and making archaeological sites in Georgia for about 12,000 years. We are still making archaeological sites today.

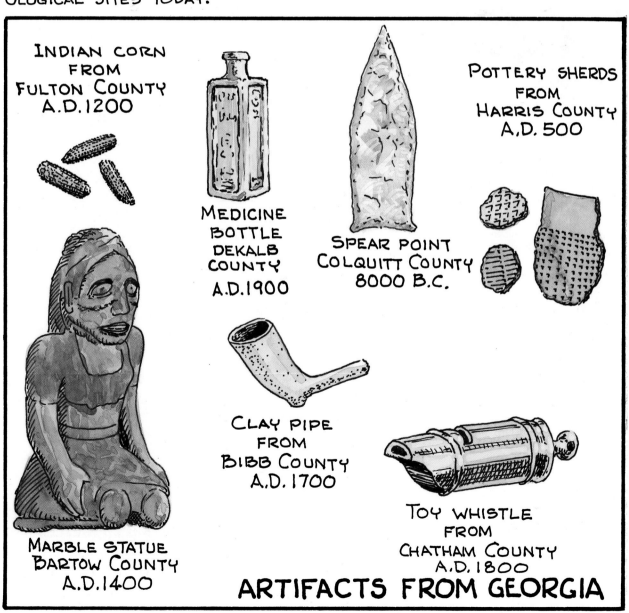

INDIAN CORN FROM FULTON COUNTY A.D. 1200

MEDICINE BOTTLE DEKALB COUNTY A.D. 1900

SPEAR POINT COLQUITT COUNTY 8000 B.C.

POTTERY SHERDS FROM HARRIS COUNTY A.D. 500

CLAY PIPE FROM BIBB COUNTY A.D. 1700

TOY WHISTLE FROM CHATHAM COUNTY A.D. 1800

MARBLE STATUE BARTOW COUNTY A.D. 1400

ARTIFACTS FROM GEORGIA

HOW DO WE CREATE ARCHAEOLOGICAL SITES? IMAGINE THAT YOU AND YOUR FAMILY HAVE GONE ON A PICNIC TO A PARK BESIDE A RIVER. YOU GET OUT OF THE CAR AND FIND A NICE PLACE FOR COOKING AND EATING. YOU SPREAD BLANKETS ON THE GROUND AND ARRANGE A CIRCLE OF STONES FOR A FIRE TO ROAST HOT DOGS. YOU OPEN SOFT DRINK CANS. YOU TALK, TELL JOKES, AND PLAY GAMES UNTIL SOMEONE YELLS THAT THE HOT DOGS ARE READY AND EVERYONE CROWDS AROUND THE FOOD. WHEN YOU FINISH EATING, YOU PLAY FOOTBALL UNTIL YOU ARE EXHAUSTED. EVERYONE SITS DOWN NEAR THE FIRE TO REST IN THE AFTERNOON SUN. LATER YOU CLEAN UP ALL YOUR TRASH, PACK UP THE BLANKETS AND COOKING UTENSILS, DOUSE THE FIRE WITH PLENTY OF WATER, AND LOAD INTO THE CAR TO RETURN HOME.

WHILE YOU MAY NEVER HAVE THOUGHT OF IT, YOUR PICNIC PRODUCED AN ARCHAEOLOGICAL SITE. THINK CAREFULLY OF THE THINGS YOU LEFT BEHIND. YOU DOUSED THE FIRE, BUT THE CHARCOAL AND ROCKS REMAINED. CHARCOAL AND STONE WILL RESIST THE WEATHER AND ARE SLOW TO DECAY. IF NO ONE DISTURBS THE FIREPLACE, THOSE ROCKS AND CHARCOAL MAY LAST FOR THOUSANDS OF YEARS. SOMEONE UNWRAPPED THE PACKAGE OF HOT DOG BUNS AND THREW THE WIRE FASTENER IN THE FIRE. THIS LITTLE WIRE WILL

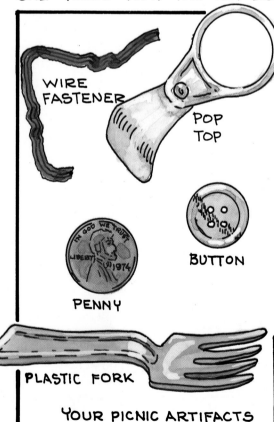

WIRE FASTENER

POP TOP

PENNY

BUTTON

PLASTIC FORK

YOUR PICNIC ARTIFACTS

LAST A VERY LONG TIME. OF COURSE, EVERYONE WAS TOLD TO THROW THE PLASTIC FORKS AND SPOONS AND THE POP TOPS FROM THE DRINK CANS INTO A TRASH BAG. DID EVERYTHING GO INTO THE BAG? SOMEONE DROPPED A PLASTIC FORK IN THE GRASS WHEN THEY WERE RUNNING AWAY FROM A BEE. SEVERAL OF THE SMALL CHILDREN DROPPED THEIR POP TOPS WHERE THEY PULLED THEM OFF. SUPPOSE, ALSO, THAT YOU LOST A BUTTON FROM YOUR SHIRT. SOMEONE ELSE LOST A PENNY DATED 1974.

NOW, IMAGINE SOMEONE IN THE FUTURE VISITING YOUR PICNIC SITE. IF THEY WERE JUST CASUALLY WALKING BY THEY MIGHT NOT SEE ANY EVIDENCE OF YOUR ACTIVITY. HOWEVER, IF AN ARCHAEOLOGIST INVESTIGATED THE SITE, HE WOULD LOOK VERY CAREFULLY FOR LOST AND DISCARDED ARTIFACTS. HE MIGHT DIG AWAY THE TOP FEW INCHES OF SOIL AND SIFT IT THROUGH A FINE SCREEN. HE WOULD FIND THE WIRE FASTENER, THE POP TOPS, THE BUTTON, AND THE COIN. SINCE THE CHARCOAL AND ROCKS ARE <u>ASSOCIATED</u> (FOUND TOGETHER), THE ARCHAEOLOGIST WOULD KNOW THAT THIS FIRE WAS MADE BY PEOPLE AND WAS NOT THE RESULT OF AN ACCIDENT SUCH AS A FOREST FIRE. FINDING OTHER ARTIFACTS NEAR THE FIRE WOULD SUGGEST THAT THEY WERE ALL PART OF THE SAME <u>CONTEXT</u> (GROUP OF ARTIFACTS). FROM THIS SMALL COLLECTION OF ARTIFACTS AND THE FIREPLACE, HE WOULD KNOW THAT THE SITE HAD NOT BEEN OCCUPIED VERY LONG. HE MIGHT DECIDE THAT SOMETIME DURING OR AFTER 1974, A SMALL GROUP OF PEOPLE CAME TO THIS SPOT, BUILT A FIRE, DRANK CANNED BEVERAGES, AND ATE FOOD. IN THIS WAY, THE ARCHAEOLOGIST WOULD BE FINDING OUT ABOUT YOUR WAY OF LIFE. OF COURSE, TO FIND OUT THE WHOLE STORY ABOUT YOU, HE WOULD HAVE TO LOOK AT SITES OTHER THAN THE PICNIC.

SUPPOSE THE ARCHAEOLOGIST DECIDED TO DIG DEEPER. AFTER DIGGING THROUGH THE TOP <u>STRATUM</u> (LAYER OF SOIL) THAT CONTAINED YOUR ARTIFACTS, HE DUG THROUGH SOME SAND THAT WAS DEPOSITED WHEN THE RIVER FLOODED IN THE PAST. BELOW THE SAND, THE ARCHAEOLOGIST FOUND A THIN STRATUM OF DARK SOIL. IN THIS SOIL HE DISCOVERED ANOTHER CIRCLE OF ROCKS WITH CHARCOAL AND DEER BONES INSIDE THE CIRCLE. OUTSIDE THE CIRCLE OF ROCKS HE FOUND BROKEN PIECES OF INDIAN POTTERY AS WELL AS AN ARROWHEAD AND SOME SMALL PIECES OF STONE. THE ARTIFACTS IN THIS SECOND ARCHAEOLOGICAL CONTEXT CLEARLY SHOW THAT LONG AGO, INDIANS COOKED AND ATE MEALS ON THE SAME SPOT THAT YOU USED FOR YOUR PICNIC.

PICNIC STRATUM
SAND STRATUM
PREHISTORIC INDIAN STRATUM

ARCHAEOLOGICAL ROBOT OF THE FUTURE.

THE WAY OF LIFE OF ANY GROUP OF PEOPLE IS CALLED THEIR <u>CULTURE</u>. PEOPLE FIRST CAME TO NORTH AMERICA FROM ASIA ABOUT 25,000 YEARS AGO. THIS WAS DURING THE ICE AGE WHEN THE WEATHER WAS COLDER THAN IT IS NOW. ANIMALS HAD ADAPTED TO THE ICE AGE BY GROWING THICK FUR. PEOPLE, ON THE OTHER HAND, DID NOT CHANGE THEIR BODIES TO SURVIVE THE COLD. INSTEAD, THEY CHANGED THEIR CULTURE TO ADAPT TO THE COLD CLIMATE. THEY BUILT FIRES, MADE CLOTHING, BUILT SNUG SHELTERS, AND COOPERATED WITH ONE ANOTHER IN THE SEARCH FOR FOOD.

ARCHAEOLOGISTS ARE INTERESTED IN THE DIFFERENT KINDS OF CULTURES THAT PEOPLE HAVE DEVELOPED IN DIFFERENT TIMES AND IN DIFFERENT PLACES.

IN MODERN AMERICAN CULTURE, WE ARE VERY DEPENDENT ON <u>TECHNOLOGY</u> AND ON THE <u>SPECIALIZED TASKS</u> OF PEOPLE WHO DO NOT EVEN KNOW ONE ANOTHER.

FARMERS IN IOWA USE HUGE MACHINES TO GATHER WHEAT. IT IS THEN SHIPPED TO A MILL TO BE GROUND INTO FLOUR.

IN ATLANTA, AT A BAKERY, THE FLOUR IS BAKED INTO THOUSANDS OF LOAVES OF BREAD.

PEOPLE IN YOUR TOWN BUY SOME OF THIS BREAD AT A GROCERY STORE AND TAKE IT HOME TO EAT.

IN OTHER CULTURES, <u>KINSHIP TIES</u> AND <u>COOPERATION</u> BETWEEN MEMBERS OF THE SAME SOCIAL GROUP ARE VERY IMPORTANT. TECH-NOLOGY AND SPECIALIZATION ARE LESS IMPORTANT.

THE FAMILY GATHERS ACORNS, AND THEN...

THEY PEEL AND GRIND THE ACORNS TO MAKE FLOUR, AND FINALLY...

THE SAME FAMILY BAKES AND EATS THE ACORN BREAD!

WHY HAVE PEOPLE DEVELOPED DIFFERENT CULTURES? THIS IS ONE OF THE MAIN QUESTIONS ARCHAEOLOGISTS ARE TRYING TO ANSWER. WHY DO SOME PEOPLE PRACTICE AGRICULTURE WHILE OTHERS GAIN A LIVING FROM HUNTING AND FISHING? WHY DO SOME CULTURES HAVE A SIMPLE RELIGION WHILE OTHERS BUILD TEMPLES AND WORSHIP MANY GODS? WHY DO SOME CULTURES MAKE THEIR TOOLS FROM STONE WHILE OTHERS HAVE LEARNED THE ART OF SMELTING IRON? HOW HAVE PEOPLE ADAPTED TO DIFFERENT ENVIRONMENTS, RANGING FROM HOT DESERTS AND JUNGLES OF THE EQUATOR TO FROZEN TUNDRA OF THE FAR NORTH? ARCHAEOLOGISTS MUST INVESTIGATE MANY PAST CULTURES BEFORE THEY CAN ATTEMPT TO ANSWER THESE QUESTIONS.

WHEN ARCHAEOLOGISTS FIND ENOUGH ARTIFACTS IN THE SAME CONTEXT AND IN ASSOCIATION WITH ONE ANOTHER, THEY CAN BEGIN TO RECONSTRUCT A CULTURE. THESE CULTURAL RECONSTRUCTIONS MUST BE CARRIED OUT CAREFULLY, AND THEY MUST BE BASED ON MANY TYPES OF INFORMATION. IF SEEDS AND NUT SHELLS ARE FOUND IN THE GARBAGE PITS OF A PARTICULAR CULTURE, THE ARCHAEOLOGISTS WILL WANT TO KNOW THE NAMES OF THE PLANTS THAT PRODUCED THESE SEEDS AND NUTS. IN ORDER TO GET THIS INFORMATION, THE ARCHAEOLOGISTS WILL CALL UPON...

A <u>BOTANIST</u> TO IDENTIFY THE PLANTS THEY FIND,

A <u>GEOLOGIST</u> TO IDENTIFY THE KINDS OF ROCKS USED FOR TOOLS IN CERTAIN CULTURES,

AND A <u>ZOOLOGIST</u> TO IDENTIFY THE BONES OF FOOD ANIMALS.

ARCHAEOLOGISTS WORK WITH SPECIALISTS IN MANY DIFFERENT SCIENCES. THIS IS CALLED THE <u>MULTIDISCIPLINARY APPROACH.</u>

IN SOME AREAS OF THE WORLD, ARCHAEOLOGISTS HAVE RECON- STRUCTED MANY CULTURES. SOME OF THESE ARE <u>PREHISTORIC</u> (BEFORE WRITING WAS USED) AND SOME ARE <u>HISTORIC</u> (AFTER WRITING). SINCE ARCHAEOLOGISTS ARE INTERESTED IN HOW ONE CULTURE CHANGES INTO ANOTHER, THEY NEED TO KNOW THE <u>CHRONOLOGY</u> (RELATIONSHIP IN TIME) OF THESE CULTURES. HISTORIC CULTURES CAN BE ASSIGNED AN AGE FROM INFORMATION IN WRITTEN RECORDS, IF EVENTS WERE RECORDED BY USE OF A CALENDAR AS WE DO. PREHISTORIC CULTURES HAD NO WRITTEN RECORDS, SO THEY ARE MUCH MORE DIFFICULT TO PLACE IN TIME.

PHYSICISTS HAVE LEARNED HOW TO TELL THE AGE OF ARTIFACTS BY A TECHNIQUE CALLED <u>RADIOCARBON DATING.</u> THIS TECHNIQUE MEASURES THE AMOUNT OF RADIOACTIVE CARBON (C_{14}) IN PIECES OF ORGANIC MATERIAL SUCH AS WOOD, BONE OR SHELL. SINCE ANCIENT PEOPLE USED WOOD FOR MANY PURPOSES AND DISCARDED BONE AND SHELL FROM THEIR MEALS, THESE MATERIALS ARE OFTEN FOUND ON ARCHAEOLOGICAL SITES. WHEN ANY LIVING THING DIES, IT BEGINS TO LOSE THE RADIOACTIVE CARBON THAT IT CONTAINS. THIS LOSS CAN BE MEASURED. THE SMALLER THE AMOUNT OF RADIOACTIVE CARBON, THE OLDER IS THE ARTIFACT. WHEN A PHYSICIST GIVES THE ARCHAEOLOGIST A DATE FOR HIS ARTIFACT, THERE IS ALWAYS A MARGIN FOR ERROR. FOR EXAMPLE, A REPORTED DATE MIGHT READ "1200 B.C. PLUS OR MINUS 200 YEARS." THIS MEANS THAT THE ARCHAEOLOGIST CAN BE REASONABLY SURE THAT HIS ARTIFACT WAS DISCARDED BETWEEN 1000 AND 1400 B.C. (1200 MINUS 200 = 1000; 1200 PLUS 200 = 1400).

RADIOCARBON IS AN <u>ABSOLUTE</u> DATING TECHNIQUE. THAT MEANS THAT THE TECHNIQUE GIVES AN AGE IN YEARS. <u>RELATIVE</u> DATING TECHNIQUES CAN BE USED TO FIND OUT IF ONE CULTURE IS OLDER OR YOUNGER THAN ANOTHER, BUT THEY DO NOT GIVE A SPECIFIC YEAR. THE MOST USED TECHNIQUE FOR RELATIVE DATING IS <u>STRATIGRAPHY.</u> IN THIS TECHNIQUE, THE ARCHAEOLOGIST OBSERVES THE SOIL STRATUM IN WHICH ARTIFACTS ARE FOUND. THE DEEPER THE STRATUM, THE OLDER IT IS.

ABOUT A.D. 1890

ANOTHER WAY OF DETERMINING THE RELATIVE AGE OF ARTIFACTS—AND CULTURES—IS BY THE USE OF TYPOLOGY. ALL OF US USE THIS TECHNIQUE EVERY DAY. WHEN WE LOOK AT AN OLD PHOTOGRAPH, WE CAN QUICKLY GUESS ITS AGE FROM THE STYLES OF DRESS, OR EVEN FROM THE HAIR STYLES. WE USE IT WHEN WE ESTIMATE THE AGE OF AN AUTOMOBILE BY THE SHAPE OF THE HOOD OR THE FENDERS.

ABOUT A.D. 1978

ARCHAEOLOGISTS HAVE LEARNED THAT PEOPLE OF THE SAME CULTURE WILL ALMOST ALWAYS MAKE THEIR TOOLS, DECORATE THEIR POTTERY, AND BUILD THEIR HOUSES IN SIMILAR WAYS. WHEN WE FIND A NUMBER OF STONE PROJECTILE POINTS (SPEAR POINTS OR ARROWHEADS) MADE IN THE SAME SHAPE AND STYLE, WE CAN BE REASONABLY SAFE IN SAYING THAT THEY WERE MADE BY PEOPLE OF SIMILAR CULTURES. A PARTICULAR STYLE OF PROJECTILE POINT CAN THEN BE LABELED A TYPE AND GIVEN A NAME.

ABOUT A.D. 1962

ABOUT A.D. 1925

ONE TYPE OF ANCIENT GEORGIA SPEAR POINT IS CALLED A "SAVANNAH RIVER POINT." THIS TYPE OF POINT WAS FIRST DISCOVERED AT SITES NEAR THE SAVANNAH RIVER. RADIOCARBON DATES OF CHARCOAL ASSOCIATED WITH THESE POINTS TELL US THAT SAVANNAH RIVER POINTS WERE MADE ABOUT 2000 B.C. (4000 YEARS AGO). NOW, WHENEVER WE FIND A POINT OF SIMILAR SHAPE, FROM SOME OTHER PART OF GEORGIA, WE CAN ESTIMATE ITS AGE BY TYPOLOGY.

TWO OLDER PROJECTILE POINT TYPES FROM SITES IN GEORGIA ARE THE "MORROW MOUNTAIN" POINT (MADE ABOUT 4000 B.C.), AND THE "PALMER" POINT (MADE ABOUT 6000 B.C.). HOW MANY THINGS IN OUR OWN CULTURE CAN YOU ESTIMATE AS TO AGE BY THEIR SHAPE AND STYLE?

SAVANNAH RIVER POINT

ABOUT 2000 B.C.

MORROW MOUNTAIN POINT

ABOUT 4000 B.C.

PALMER POINT

ABOUT 6000 B.C.

Now that you know what archaeology is, you will want to find out more about the things archaeologists have learned in their studies of the past cultures in Georgia. Also, you will be curious about how archaeologists conduct their research in the field and in the laboratory. These are the subjects of the rest of this book.

Before we go on, however, it is important that you understand the serious and urgent need for preserving the archaeological resources of Georgia. Many of these resources—sites and the artifacts they contain—are in danger of being destroyed. If they are destroyed before they can be studied by archaeologists, the information is lost forever. Each archaeological site is IRREPLACEABLE (unique in the information that it contains).

Sites are destroyed in two major ways. One way is through PROGRESS—the construction of houses, new roads, lakes, and shopping centers. Other sites are damaged or destroyed by VANDALISM—treasure hunting or digging by untrained artifact collectors. We must all work together to prevent vandalism of sites. Loss from progress is not as great as it used to be because there are some new state and national laws that require archaeological studies of areas where certain kinds of construction are proposed.

Sometimes individuals or groups can work to protect and preserve archaeological resources in their home areas. The citizens of some communities in Georgia have raised money to build local museums to preserve and display artifacts found in their areas. When prehistoric Indian quarry sites were in danger of being lost to progress in DeKalb County, a group of concerned citizens formed a "task force" to make county and state officials aware of the potential loss. In White County, one family has, through the years, protected the important Indian mound of Nacoochee. In 1915, this family allowed archaeologists from the Museum of the American Indian to excavate part of the mound. Afterwards, the archaeologists restored the excavated portion of the mound, and the remainder of the site has been preserved since then.

Perhaps the best example of preservation is the Etowah mounds site near Cartersville. For years, the owners refused offers from relic collectors and dealers to buy or lease the site. They waited until the site could be purchased by the State of Georgia to be preserved forever for scientific study and public education.

CONSTRUCTION

VANDALISM

KNOWLEDGE LOST

SCIENTIFIC EXCAVATION

PRESERVATION

KNOWLEDGE GAINED

CHAPTER II
GEORGIA'S PAST

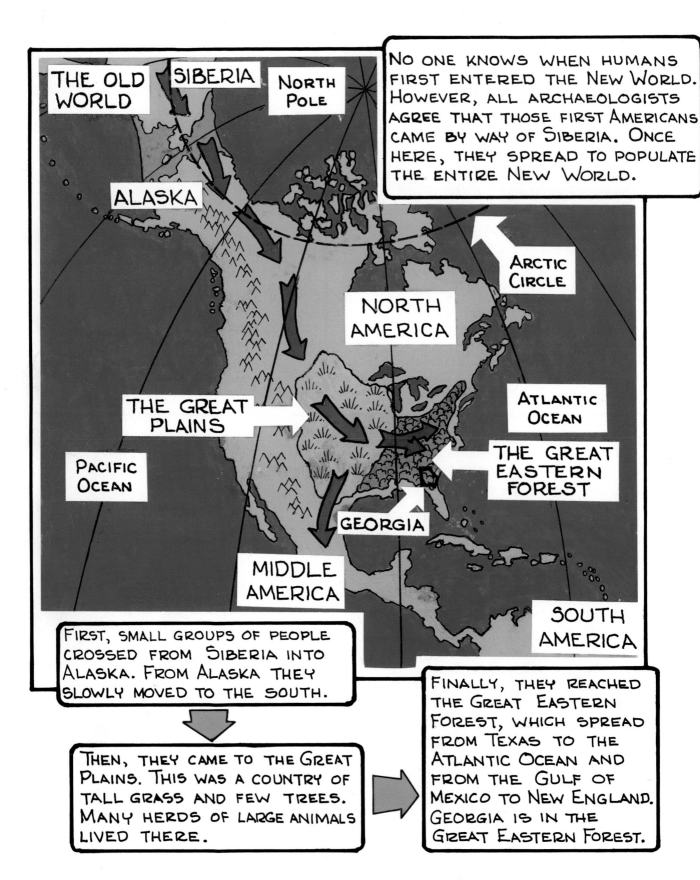

THE OLD WORLD

SIBERIA

NORTH POLE

ALASKA

No one knows when humans first entered the New World. However, all archaeologists agree that those first Americans came by way of Siberia. Once here, they spread to populate the entire New World.

ARCTIC CIRCLE

NORTH AMERICA

THE GREAT PLAINS

ATLANTIC OCEAN

THE GREAT EASTERN FOREST

PACIFIC OCEAN

GEORGIA

MIDDLE AMERICA

SOUTH AMERICA

First, small groups of people crossed from Siberia into Alaska. From Alaska they slowly moved to the south.

Then, they came to the Great Plains. This was a country of tall grass and few trees. Many herds of large animals lived there.

Finally, they reached the Great Eastern Forest, which spread from Texas to the Atlantic Ocean and from the Gulf of Mexico to New England. Georgia is in the Great Eastern Forest.

THANKS TO CARBON-14 DATING, WE KNOW THAT PEOPLE HAVE BEEN IN THE New World (NORTH, MIDDLE AND SOUTH AMERICA) FOR AT LEAST 25,000 YEARS. THERE ARE A FEW SITES IN WESTERN NORTH AMERICA THAT MAY BE AS OLD AS 50,000 YEARS. BUT THE AGE OF THESE SITES IS NOT ACCEPTED BY ALL ARCHAEOLOGISTS. ALTHOUGH WE MAY NEVER KNOW EXACTLY WHEN THE FIRST SIBERIAN PEOPLE CAME INTO THE NEW WORLD, WE DO KNOW THAT THESE MIGRATIONS TOOK PLACE DURING THE Pleistocene Epoch (ICE AGE). AT THAT TIME THE SEA LEVEL WAS MUCH LOWER, AND ASIA AND AMERICA WERE CONNECTED BY LAND. THOSE EARLY SIBERIANS WALKED INTO THE NEW WORLD ON DRY LAND. THIS "LAND BRIDGE," SHOWN IN BROWN ON THE MAP (PAGE 12), EXISTED UNTIL ABOUT 15,000 YEARS AGO.

ARCHAEOLOGISTS CALL THESE EARLY PEOPLE Paleo Indians. THE NAME "INDIAN" WAS GIVEN BY COLUMBUS TO THE NATIVES THAT HE FOUND IN AMERICA BECAUSE HE THOUGHT HE HAD DIS-COVERED A NEW ROUTE TO INDIA. ARCHAEOLOGISTS BELIEVE THAT THE PEOPLE DISCOVERED BY COLUMBUS WERE DESCENDANTS OF THOSE FIRST MIGRANTS FROM SIBERIA.

INDIANS HAVE BEEN IN THE EASTERN PART OF NORTH AMERICA FOR AT LEAST 18,000 YEARS. THE FIRST INDIAN SETTLERS IN THE EASTERN FOREST PROBABLY CAME FROM THE GREAT PLAINS. THERE, THEY HAD SPENT MUCH OF THEIR TIME HUNTING LARGE ANIMALS SUCH AS MAMMOTHS AND BISON. IN THE EASTERN FOREST, THERE WERE FEW HERDS OF THESE LARGE ANIMALS, SO THE PALEO INDIANS HAD TO ADAPT (CHANGE THEIR CULTURE) BY HUNTING SMALLER GAME SUCH AS DEER AND TURKEY AND BY COLLECTING A WIDE VARIETY OF FOOD PLANTS. SINCE THE FOREST WAS VERY DIFFERENT FROM THE GREAT PLAINS, THE INDIANS HAD MANY ADAPTATIONS TO MAKE. THEY LEARNED EVERY FACET OF THE FOREST ENVIRONMENT. THEY INVENTED NEW TYPES OF TOOLS AND SHELTERS, AND THEY CHANGED THE ORGANIZATION OF THEIR SOCIETY.

THE AREA WE NOW CALL GEORGIA WAS INHABITED BY PALEO-INDIANS BY 10,000 B.C. AS TODAY, ALL PARTS OF GEORGIA WERE NOT ALIKE. IT WAS NECESSARY FOR THE PALEO INDIANS TO ADJUST TO DIFFERENCES OF THE MOUNTAINS, PIEDMONT, AND COASTAL PLAIN.

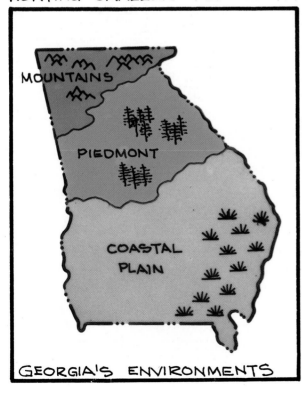

MOUNTAINS

PIEDMONT

COASTAL PLAIN

GEORGIA'S ENVIRONMENTS

PALEO INDIAN PERIOD
10,000 B.C. TO 8,000 B.C.

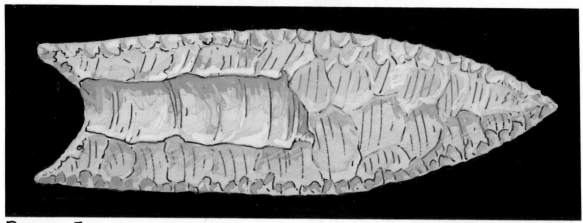

PALEO INDIAN HUNTERS MADE BEAUTIFUL <u>LANCEOLATE</u> (LANCE-SHAPED) SPEAR POINTS LIKE THE CLOVIS POINT SHOWN ABOVE. BONE AND STONE TOOLS WERE USED TO CHIP THE POINTS TO A PRECISE SHAPE. THIS SHAPE WAS DESIGNED TO FORM A DURABLE STONE TIP TO A LONG, WOODEN SHAFT LIKE THE ONE SHOWN BELOW.

SUCH A SPEAR WAS IDEAL FOR USE AS A THRUSTING WEAPON. THE HUNTER DROVE OR THRUST HIS SPEAR INTO THE ANIMAL. SINCE IT WAS JOINED SMOOTHLY TO THE SHAFT, THERE WERE NO BARBS TO HANG UP IN THE ANIMAL AND IT COULD BE PULLED OUT EASILY AND DRIVEN IN AGAIN. A HEAVY WEAPON LIKE THIS WOULD NOT BE SUITABLE FOR HUNTING THE SWIFT DEER, BUT IT WAS IDEAL FOR USE ON LARGE, SLOW-MOVING ANIMALS LIKE GROUND SLOTHS, BISON, AND MASTODONS, OCCASSIONALLY FOUND IN GEORGIA.

LARGE PLEISTOCENE ANIMALS OF GEORGIA.

IN WESTERN NORTH AMERICA, ARCHAEOLOGISTS HAVE FOUND MANY SITES OF PALEO INDIAN HUNTERS WHERE WEAPONS, TOOLS AND THE BONES OF LARGE ANIMALS ARE CLEARLY ASSOCIATED. IN THE EASTERN STATES, THE SAME WEAPONS AND TOOLS ARE FOUND, BUT THE ANIMAL BONES ARE USUALLY MISSING. PRESERVATION OF <u>ORGANIC MATERIAL</u> (BONES, WOOD AND LEATHER) IS NOT VERY GOOD IN THE EAST BECAUSE OF THE WETTER CLIMATE. ARCHAEOLOGISTS MUST CONTINUE TO SEARCH FOR SITES IN GEORGIA AND OTHER EASTERN STATES WHERE THE BONES OF ANIMALS, AS WELL AS STONE ARTIFACTS, MIGHT BE PRESERVED.

FLINT AND CHERT WERE THE FAVORITE TYPES OF STONE USED IN MAKING SPEAR POINTS AND TOOLS. THESE STONES ARE PLENTIFUL IN NORTHWEST GEORGIA AS WELL AS ON THE COASTAL PLAIN, BUT THEY DO NOT OCCUR ON THE PIEDMONT. STONE POINTS AND TOOLS ON THE PIEDMONT WERE USUALLY MADE OF QUARTZ.

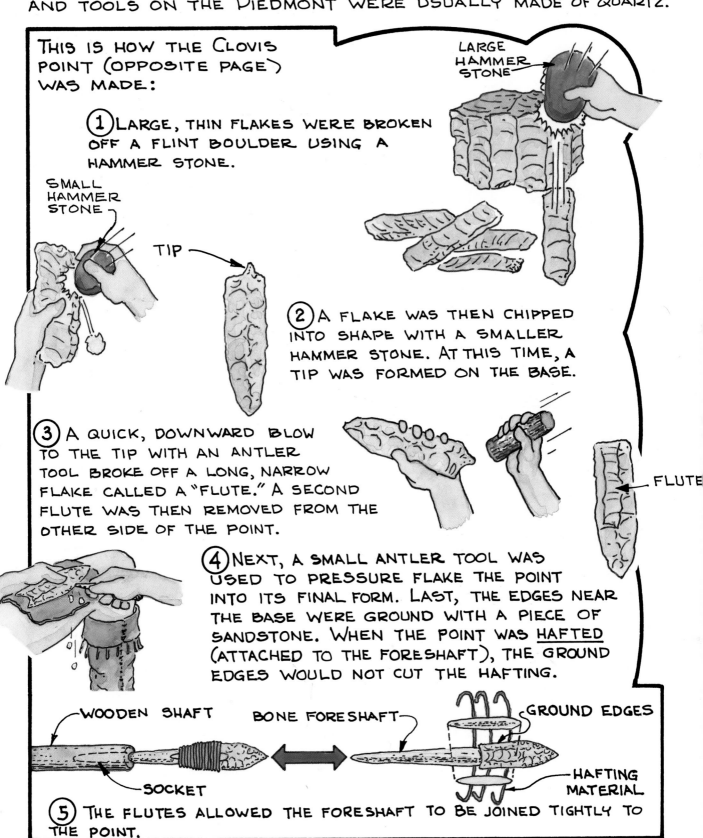

THIS IS HOW THE CLOVIS POINT (OPPOSITE PAGE) WAS MADE:

LARGE HAMMER STONE

(1) LARGE, THIN FLAKES WERE BROKEN OFF A FLINT BOULDER USING A HAMMER STONE.

SMALL HAMMER STONE

TIP

(2) A FLAKE WAS THEN CHIPPED INTO SHAPE WITH A SMALLER HAMMER STONE. AT THIS TIME, A TIP WAS FORMED ON THE BASE.

(3) A QUICK, DOWNWARD BLOW TO THE TIP WITH AN ANTLER TOOL BROKE OFF A LONG, NARROW FLAKE CALLED A "FLUTE." A SECOND FLUTE WAS THEN REMOVED FROM THE OTHER SIDE OF THE POINT.

FLUTE

(4) NEXT, A SMALL ANTLER TOOL WAS USED TO PRESSURE FLAKE THE POINT INTO ITS FINAL FORM. LAST, THE EDGES NEAR THE BASE WERE GROUND WITH A PIECE OF SANDSTONE. WHEN THE POINT WAS <u>HAFTED</u> (ATTACHED TO THE FORESHAFT), THE GROUND EDGES WOULD NOT CUT THE HAFTING.

WOODEN SHAFT   BONE FORESHAFT   GROUND EDGES

SOCKET   HAFTING MATERIAL

(5) THE FLUTES ALLOWED THE FORESHAFT TO BE JOINED TIGHTLY TO THE POINT.

PALEO INDIAN HUNTERS OF THE WESTERN PLAINS ATTACKING A MAMMOTH.

TO THE ARCHAEOLOGIST, LANCEOLATE POINTS ARE MUCH MORE THAN
BEAUTIFUL STONE WORK. THESE SPEAR POINTS ARE THE REMAINS OF A
SPECIAL KIND OF CULTURE. HERE ARE SOME OF THE THINGS WE CAN SAY
ABOUT PALEO INDIAN CULTURE: PALEO INDIANS WERE HUNTER-GATHERERS.
BY THIS WE MEAN THAT THEY HUNTED WILD ANIMALS AND GATHERED WILD
PLANTS. THEY KNEW NOTHING ABOUT THE USE OF METALS. THEREFORE,
THEIR TOOLS AND WEAPONS WERE MADE OF STONE, BONE, OR WOOD.
PALEO INDIANS LIVED IN SMALL, NOMADIC (WANDERING) GROUPS. ALL
THE MEMBERS OF A GROUP WERE RELATED BY KINSHIP. WE CALL THIS
TYPE OF FAMILY GROUP A "BAND." A BAND HAD FROM 25 TO 50 MEMBERS.

PALEO INDIANS HAD A RELIGION CALLED "ANIMISM." ANIMISM MEANS
THAT EVERYTHING WAS GIVEN LIFE (ANIMATED). ROCKS, RIVERS, THE GROUND,

THE WIND, THE SUN—ALL HAD SPIRITS OR SOULS. THESE SPIRITS HAD HUMAN QUALITIES. THEY COULD SEE, HEAR, TOUCH, AND SMELL. THEY COULD BE HAPPY, SAD, OR ANGRY. IN ADDITION, THEY HAD MAGICAL QUALITIES. EVEN THOUGH THEY WERE INVISIBLE, THEY COULD BRING GOOD OR BAD FORTUNE TO PEOPLE. BUT THE SPIRITS COULD BE BROUGHT UNDER HUMAN CONTROL. FOR EXAMPLE, A HUNTER MIGHT PUT CERTAIN ANIMAL SPIRITS UNDER A MAGIC SPELL SO THAT THE REAL ANIMALS WOULD BE EASIER TO KILL.

ILLNESS WAS A VERY SERIOUS MATTER. A SICK PERSON MIGHT HAVE OFFENDED AN ANIMAL HE HAD KILLED; OR SOMEONE WHO HATED HIM MIGHT HAVE PUT AN EVIL SPELL ON HIM. TO TAKE CARE OF SUCH PROBLEMS, EVERY BAND HAD A <u>SHAMAN.</u> SHAMANS KNEW HOW TO USE MANY KINDS OF MAGIC SPELLS AND CURES. SOMETIMES THE SHAMAN HAD TO GO INTO A TRANCE SO THAT HE COULD COMMUNICATE WITH THE SPIRITS. WHEN THE SHAMAN AWOKE, HE WOULD PERFORM A RITUAL TO DRIVE AWAY THE EVIL SPIRIT THAT WAS THE CAUSE OF THE ILLNESS.

EACH BAND HAD LEGENDS ABOUT THE CREATION OF THE WORLD; HOW PEOPLE BECAME SUPERIOR TO ANIMALS, HOW EACH USEFUL PLANT ORIGINATED, HOW THE SUN AND MOON WERE PLACED IN THE SKY, AND MANY MORE. STORYTELLERS IN EVERY BAND TOLD THESE LEGENDS REGULARLY SO THAT EVERY MEMBER, ESPECIALLY CHILDREN, COULD LEARN AND BENEFIT FROM THEM.

PALEO INDIANS MADE USE OF MANY TYPES OF FOOD. MEAT OF ANIMALS KILLED BY THE HUNTERS WAS THE MAIN SOURCE OF FOOD. ONE OF THE OLDER MEN WAS LEADER OF THE HUNTERS. THE LIFE OR DEATH OF THE BAND DEPENDED ON THE SKILL OF THESE HUNTERS. MANY DIFFERENT PLANTS WERE ALSO EATEN. THERE WERE NUTS, BERRIES, FRUITS, ROOTS, SEEDS, AND BARK THAT COULD BE EATEN. PLANTS WERE COLLECTED BY THE WOMEN AND CHILDREN OF THE BAND. SOME PLANTS WERE POISONOUS. THESE PLANTS WERE THOUGHT TO HAVE EVIL SPIRITS THAT HATED PEOPLE.

Paleo Indians had a social system that kept the family together. The purpose of the family unit was to give protection and care to the young, who were helpless during their early years. Several related families, usually brothers, their wives and children, made up a band. Each member of a band had **specific tasks**. In this way, even small children made a contribution to the welfare of the group. But more important, children grew up as an integral part of the family and the band. A child was thought to be grown at age 12 or 13, and, at that time, he or she was initiated into adulthood by an elaborate ceremony. Soon after this, these children could marry.

Paleo Indians knew how to protect themselves from the weather. They cut and sewed clothing from the skins of animals they hunted. They made small shelters that were held up by bones and sticks and were covered with animal skins. These shelters kept out the harsh weather and kept in the warmth. Paleo Indians knew how to make fire for heat, light, and cooking. Each day, there was much work to be done. Cooperation was essential between the members of a Paleo Indian band.

A Paleo Indian band.

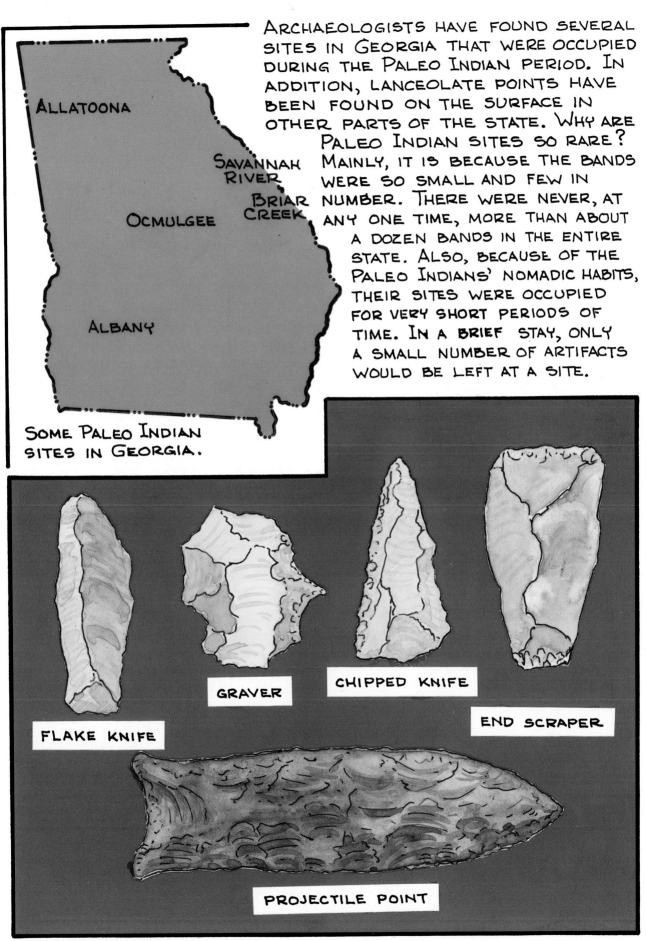

SOME PALEO INDIAN SITES IN GEORGIA.

ARCHAEOLOGISTS HAVE FOUND SEVERAL SITES IN GEORGIA THAT WERE OCCUPIED DURING THE PALEO INDIAN PERIOD. IN ADDITION, LANCEOLATE POINTS HAVE BEEN FOUND ON THE SURFACE IN OTHER PARTS OF THE STATE. WHY ARE PALEO INDIAN SITES SO RARE? MAINLY, IT IS BECAUSE THE BANDS WERE SO SMALL AND FEW IN NUMBER. THERE WERE NEVER, AT ANY ONE TIME, MORE THAN ABOUT A DOZEN BANDS IN THE ENTIRE STATE. ALSO, BECAUSE OF THE PALEO INDIANS' NOMADIC HABITS, THEIR SITES WERE OCCUPIED FOR VERY SHORT PERIODS OF TIME. IN A BRIEF STAY, ONLY A SMALL NUMBER OF ARTIFACTS WOULD BE LEFT AT A SITE.

FLAKE KNIFE

GRAVER

CHIPPED KNIFE

END SCRAPER

PROJECTILE POINT

PALEO INDIAN STONE ARTIFACTS FROM GEORGIA

ARCHAIC INDIAN PERIOD
8,000 B.C. TO 1,000 B.C.

AFTER 8,000 B.C., WE USE THE NAME "ARCHAIC INDIAN" TO DESCRIBE THE PEOPLE LIVING IN GEORGIA. THESE PEOPLE WERE DESCENDENTS OF THE PALEO INDIANS. ARCHAEOLOGISTS GIVE THEM A DIFFERENT NAME BECAUSE THEIR CULTURE WAS BEGINNING TO CHANGE. THE ICY PLEISTOCENE EPOCH HAD COME TO A CLOSE AND THE EVIRONMENT OF EASTERN NORTH AMERICA WAS BECOMING MUCH LIKE IT IS TODAY.

ARCHAIC INDIANS, LIKE THEIR PALEO INDIAN FOREFATHERS, WERE STILL NOMADIC HUNTER-GATHERERS. THEIR RELIGION WAS STILL ANIMISM. THEY STILL LIVED IN BANDS. BUT THERE WAS ONE BIG DIFFERENCE. THE FEW LARGE ANIMALS LIKE MASTODONS, GROUND SLOTHS, AND GIANT BISON, HAD BECOME <u>EXTINCT</u> (DIED OUT) BY 8,000 B.C. ON ARCHAIC SITES, WE FIND SOME VERY DISTINCTIVE ARTIFACTS. THESE ARTIFACTS TELL AN INTERESTING STORY OF HOW PEOPLE'S LIVES WERE CHANGING IN THE FOREST.

PALEO INDIAN

ARCHAIC INDIAN

WOODLAND INDIAN

MISSISSIPPIAN INDIAN

HISTORIC INDIAN AND EUROPEAN

TIME

ARCHAEOLOGICAL PERIODS IN GEORGIA

CRACK!

THE PROJECTILE POINT ABOVE IS A
LANCEOLATE POINT, BUT YOU WILL NOTICE THAT
IT HAS NOTCHES ON THE SIDES. THIS SIDE-
NOTCHING TELLS US THAT THESE POINTS WERE
ATTACHED TO SMALLER SPEARS WHICH
WERE THROWN LIKE JAVELINS.

NOW, THE PEOPLE WERE HUNTING DEER,
BEAR, AND SMALLER ANIMALS. TO HUNT THOSE
ANIMALS, THEY HAD TO HURL THEIR SPEARS.
THIS WOULD HAVE CAUSED THE SPEAR POINTS
TO BREAK MORE OFTEN THAN WITH THE
EARLIER THRUSTING SPEAR. A BROKEN SPEAR
POINT WAS OF LITTLE USE TO A HUNTER FAR
FROM HIS HOME, SO HE RECHIPPED THE
BROKEN POINT WHILE IT WAS STILL ATTACHED
TO THE SHAFT. SOMETIMES A POINT WOULD
BE REWORKED TWO OR THREE TIMES.

TIK
A
TIK
A
TIK
A
TIK

SOMETIME DURING THE EARLY PART OF THE ARCHAIC PERIOD, HUNTERS DISCOVERED A NEW AND BETTER WAY TO HURL THEIR SPEARS. THIS INVENTION IS CALLED A "SPEAR THROWER." IN EFFECT, THE SPEAR THROWER ADDS A THIRD LINK TO THE ARM. IT ALLOWS THE HUNTER TO THROW HIS SPEAR WITH MORE POWER AND ACCURACY.

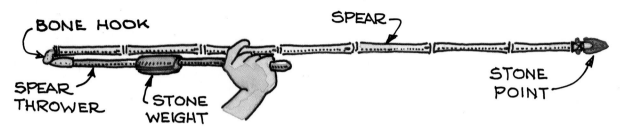

BONE HOOK
SPEAR
STONE POINT
SPEAR THROWER
STONE WEIGHT

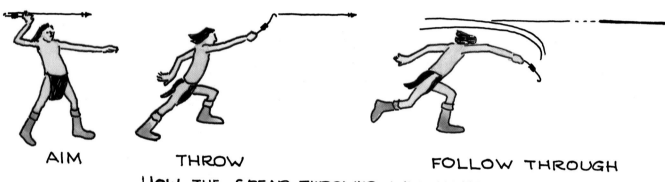

AIM   THROW   FOLLOW THROUGH

How THE SPEAR THROWER WAS USED.

ARCHAEOLOGISTS HAVE FOUND PARTS OF SPEAR THROWERS AT SITES AS OLD AS ABOUT 5,000 B.C. THE HOOKS WERE MADE FROM BONE OR DEER ANTLER AND THERE WAS A POLISHED STONE WEIGHT IN THE MIDDLE OF THE STICK. ARCHAEOLOGISTS DO NOT KNOW FOR SURE WHY THE STONE WEIGHTS WERE USED. IT MAY BE THAT THEY HELPED TO BALANCE THE HEAVY SPEAR PRIOR TO THE THROW. SOME OF THE WEIGHTS HAVE UNUSUAL SHAPES, LIKE THOSE SHOWN BELOW.

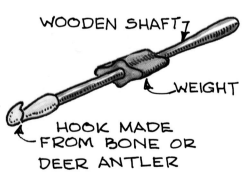

WOODEN SHAFT
WEIGHT
HOOK MADE FROM BONE OR DEER ANTLER

DURING THE <u>EARLY ARCHAIC PERIOD</u> (8,000 B.C. TO 4,000 B.C.), THE INDIANS OF GEORGIA BECAME WELL ADAPTED TO LIFE IN THE FOREST. BUT IN THE <u>LATE ARCHAIC PERIOD</u> (4,000 B.C. TO 1,000 B.C.), THEY TRULY BECAME MASTERS OF THE FOREST.

NOTHING SHOWS THIS MASTERY OF THE FOREST BETTER THAN THE <u>GROOVED AXE</u>, WHICH BECAME A COMMON TOOL AFTER ABOUT 4,000 B.C. THIS AXE HEAD WAS HAFTED TO A STRONG WOODEN HANDLE. WITH THIS TOOL, ARCHAIC INDIANS BEGAN TO CLEAR TREES FROM AREAS OF THE FOREST. WHEREVER THE FOREST WAS CLEARED, A NEW GROWTH OF BERRIES, GRAPES, PLUMS, WEEDS, AND SMALL TREES WOULD OCCUR. THESE PLANTS WERE A RICH SOURCE OF FOOD FOR THE PEOPLE. IN ADDITION, DEER AND OTHER ANIMALS CAME TO THESE CLEARINGS TO EAT THE TENDER YOUNG LEAVES AND SHOOTS. THE HUNTER NO LONGER HAD TO WANDER IN THE FOREST IN SEARCH OF GAME — THE ANIMALS NOW CAME TO <u>HIS</u> CLEARINGS!

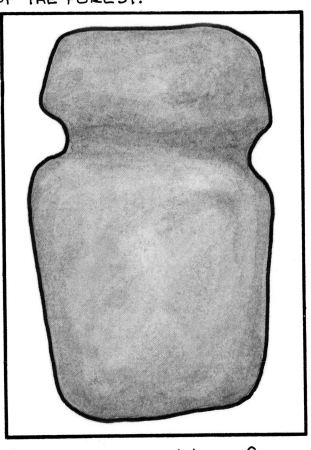

GROOVED AXE FROM WILKES COUNTY

AXE HEADS WERE MADE FROM TOUGH, CRYSTALLINE STONE. THE INDIAN USED A PEBBLE TO PECK THE AXE HEAD INTO SHAPE. THEN, HE SMOOTHED OUT MOST OF THE PECK MARKS WITH SAND-STONE. IT TOOK SEVERAL HOURS TO MAKE ONE AXE HEAD. THE EXAMPLE ABOVE WAS FOUND IN WILKES COUNTY.

LIFE IN THE LATE PART OF THE ARCHAIC PERIOD WAS VERY DIFFERENT FROM EARLY ARCHAIC AND PALEO INDIAN TIMES. POPULATIONS INCREASED GREATLY BECAUSE FOOD WAS SO PLENTIFUL IN THE FOREST, BUT WITH THE POPULATION INCREASE, BANDS COULD NO LONGER WANDER ABOUT AS FREELY AS BEFORE. GRADUALLY, EACH BAND BECAME CONFINED TO A SINGLE TERRITORY. WITH LESS LAND ON WHICH TO HUNT AND GATHER, IT WAS NECESSARY FOR PEOPLE TO TRAVEL WITHIN THE TERRITORY IN A SEASONAL PATTERN IN ORDER TO TAKE ADVANTAGE OF EACH TYPE OF FOOD RESOURCE WHEN IT WAS MOST AVAILABLE.

MEN TRAVELED AFAR TO HUNT DEER, BEAR, TURKEY, DUCK, RABBIT, SQUIRREL, FOX, RACCOON, AND OPOSSUM. NEAR THE CAMPS, WOMEN GATHERED NUTS, BERRIES, SEEDS, LEAVES, ROOTS, AND SMALL ANIMALS. IF SEASONAL MOVEMENTS BROUGHT A BAND NEAR A LARGE RIVER OR THE SEACOAST, MEN, WOMEN, AND CHILDREN WOULD FISH AND COLLECT SHELLFISH.

GRINDING STONE FOUND IN FAYETTE COUNTY.

THE GRINDING STONE WAS A TOOL OFTEN USED BY INDIANS OF THE LATE ARCHAIC PERIOD. ACORNS AND NUTS FROM THE FOREST, AND SEEDS FROM THE CLEARED LANDS WERE GATHERED IN HUGE QUANTITIES AND CRUSHED INTO FLOUR OR MEAL. A STONE PESTLE WAS USED TO CRUSH THE NUTS AND SEEDS IN THE GRINDING STONE. A GRINDING STONE WOULD BECOME HOLLOWED OUT BY THIS CONTINUED USE. A SIMILAR TOOL WAS THE NUTTING STONE. SMALL DEPRESSIONS WERE WORKED INTO THE FACE OF A ROUGH, FLAT STONE. THEN, USING A HAMMER STONE, NUTS WERE BROKEN OPEN TO EXTRACT THEIR MEAT. OIL FROM NUTS WAS USED IN COOKING.

ONE FACE OF A PESTLE WILL BE FLAT FROM WEAR.

USE MARKS

HAMMER STONES ARE ROUND. THEY WILL HAVE MANY USE MARKS ON THEM.

NUTTING STONE FOUND IN COWETA COUNTY.

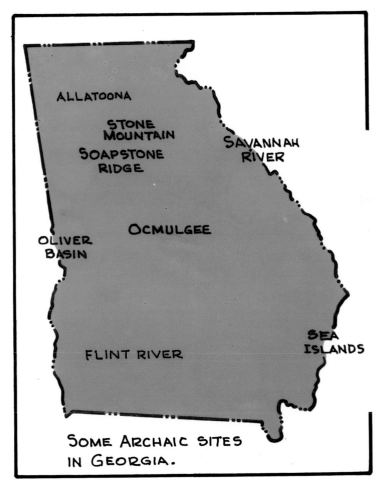

SOME ARCHAIC SITES
IN GEORGIA.

SITES OF THE ARCHAIC PERIOD ARE FOUND IN EVERY PART OF GEORGIA, FROM THE MOUNTAINS TO THE COASTAL ISLANDS. MANY OF THESE SITES HAVE REVEALED THE SEASONAL ACTIVITIES OF THE ARCHAIC PEOPLE. LARGE MOUNDS OF SEASHELLS AT SOME COASTAL SITES ARE CLEAR EVIDENCE OF THE FREQUENT USE OF SHELL-FISH AS FOOD.

ALTHOUGH SOME OF THESE COASTAL SITES MAY HAVE BEEN OCCUPIED FOR LONG PERIODS, THE PEOPLE STILL MOVED INLAND TO HUNT DEER DURING THE WINTER MONTHS. EDIBLE WILD PLANTS, SUCH AS HICKORY NUTS AND HACKBERRIES, WERE ALSO IMPORTANT IN THEIR DIETS.

SHELLFISH, SUCH AS CLAMS, OYSTERS, AND SNAILS, HAD LONG BEEN A SOURCE OF FOOD, BUT IN THE LATE ARCHAIC PERIOD, BANDS LIVING ALONG RIVERS AND ON THE SEACOAST BEGAN TO USE THIS RESOURCE IN GREATER AMOUNTS. THEY MADE HUGE SHELL "RINGS" ON THE SEA ISLANDS AND SHELL MOUNDS ALONG THE SAVANNAH RIVER.

FRESH WATER CLAM

CLAMS GROW IN MANY OF GEORGIA'S FRESH WATER STREAMS.

FRESH WATER SNAIL

THESE SHELLFISH LIVE IN MANY OF GEORGIA'S RIVERS AND CREEKS.

SALT WATER OYSTER

THESE TASTY SHELLFISH LIVE IN SHALLOW WATER ALONG GEORGIA'S COAST.

SALT WATER CONCH

ALTHOUGH THEIR MEAT WAS TOUGH, THE CONCH WAS ALSO AN IMPORTANT SEAFOOD.

By 2500 B.C., Archaic Indians were using large amounts of vegetable foods. Most vegetable foods must be cooked by boiling. Late Archaic Indians used a technique called "Stone Boiling." All it takes to stone boil are:

A fire,

Two forked sticks,

Rocks,

And, A pit lined with an animal skin which is filled with water.

The rocks were heated in the fire until they became red hot. Then, they were picked up, using the forked sticks, and dropped into the animal skin full of water. The heat from the rocks quickly brought the water to a boil. Indians prepared leaves of many wild plants just as we cook turnip greens or spinach. Wild greens were flavored with bear meat and salt to make a tasty dish.

In the Piedmont Region of Georgia (see map on page 27), there are many deposits of a type of rock called "soapstone." Soapstone has some very unusual qualities. It is soft and easy to carve. In addition, it will not break when heated. A stone like this is ideal for making cooking pots.

The bowl was hollowed out using a wooden mallet and a chisel made from a deer antler.

Blank

Soapstone boulder found in DeKalb County. A mushroom-shaped "blank" was carved out of the boulder and then was broken off.

Finished soapstone bowl found near Stone Mountain in DeKalb County.

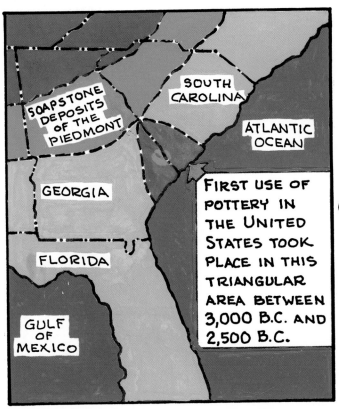

SOAPSTONE DEPOSITS OF THE PIEDMONT

SOUTH CAROLINA

ATLANTIC OCEAN

GEORGIA

FLORIDA

GULF OF MEXICO

FIRST USE OF POTTERY IN THE UNITED STATES TOOK PLACE IN THIS TRIANGULAR AREA BETWEEN 3,000 B.C. AND 2,500 B.C.

AT THE SAME TIME THAT ARCHAIC PEOPLE ON THE PIEDMONT BEGAN USING SOAPSTONE BOWLS, AN IMPORTANT DEVELOPMENT OCCURRED ON THE COAST OF GEORGIA AND SOUTH CAROLINA. INDIANS LIVING ON THE COASTAL PLAIN ALSO NEEDED COOKING POTS. THEY HAD NO SOAPSTONE DEPOSITS, SO THEY BEGAN MAKING POTTERY (CLAY POTS).

WHEN PEOPLE START MAKING COOKING POTS, THIS TELLS US TWO IMPORTANT THINGS ABOUT THEM. FIRST, OF COURSE, IS THAT THEY ARE COOKING FOODS THAT MUST BE HELD IN A CONTAINER, THAT IS, THEY ARE BOILING OR FRYING SOME OF THEIR FOODS. SECOND, PEOPLE WHO USE COOKING POTS ARE LIVING A FAIRLY SETTLED EXISTENCE, BECAUSE IT IS NOT PRACTICAL FOR WANDERING BANDS TO CARRY TOO MUCH BAGGAGE. THE APPEARANCE OF THESE POTS CONFIRMS THAT LATE ARCHAIC INDIANS WERE LIVING IN SMALLER TERRITORIES, WERE MORE SETTLED, AND WERE MAKING BETTER USE OF THE FULL RANGE OF FOODS AROUND THEM.

NORTH AMERICA

GEORGIA

SOUTH AMERICA

FIBER-TEMPERED BOWL FOUND IN CHATHAM COUNTY. SPANISH MOSS OR SOME OTHER PLANT FIBER WAS MIXED WITH THE CLAY. THESE FIBERS BURNED OUT WHEN THE POTTERY WAS BEING FIRED. AS A RESULT, THE SURFACE OF THE POT IS COVERED WITH TINY HOLES.

PRIMITIVE POTTERY WAS ALSO MADE IN SOUTH AMERICA ABOUT 3,000 B.C. THIS POTTERY IS VERY SIMILAR TO THE GEORGIA VARIETY. SOME ARCHAEOLOGISTS BELIEVE THAT KNOWLEDGE OF POTTERY-MAKING WAS BROUGHT FROM SOUTH AMERICA TO THE COAST OF GEORGIA AND SOUTH CAROLINA BY INDIAN MIGRANTS. OTHER ARCHAEOLOGISTS THINK IT WAS INDEPENDENTLY INVENTED IN BOTH PLACES.

HUNTING

GATHERING

MAKING BOWLS

MAKING FIRE

SHELLFISHING

AT THE END OF THE ARCHAIC PERIOD, THERE WERE SEVERAL THOUSAND PEOPLE LIVING IN GEORGIA. THEY HAD DEVELOPED A VERY COMPLEX CULTURE THAT WAS BASED ON USING ALL THE RICHES FOUND IN THE GREAT EASTERN FOREST. THEY HAD INVENTED POTTERY, WHICH SLOWLY SPREAD OVER ALL OF EASTERN NORTH AMERICA, AND THEY HAD LEARNED TO CLEAR LAND FOR HUNTING AND GATHERING.

THE ARCHAIC PERIOD WAS A TIME FOR LEARNING, EXPERIMENTING, GROWTH, AND ADAPTATION. BY 1,000 B.C., LIFE FOR THESE EARLY GEORGIANS HAD CHANGED SO MUCH THAT WE CAN NO LONGER CALL THEM ARCHAIC INDIANS. SO WE HAVE TO CHANGE NAMES AGAIN. THE NEXT NAME WE USE IS "WOODLAND INDIANS." BUT REMEMBER, THESE ARE NOT NEW PEOPLE. WOODLAND INDIANS WERE DESCENDANTS OF EARLIER INDIANS OF THE ARCHAIC AND PALEO INDIAN PERIODS.

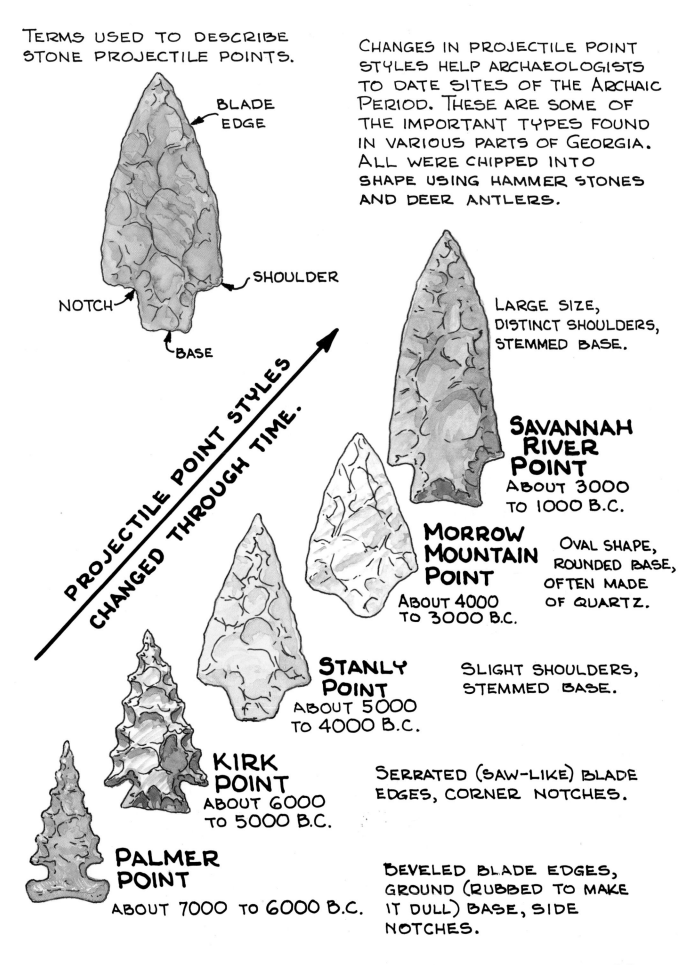

TERMS USED TO DESCRIBE STONE PROJECTILE POINTS.

BLADE EDGE

SHOULDER

NOTCH

BASE

CHANGES IN PROJECTILE POINT STYLES HELP ARCHAEOLOGISTS TO DATE SITES OF THE ARCHAIC PERIOD. THESE ARE SOME OF THE IMPORTANT TYPES FOUND IN VARIOUS PARTS OF GEORGIA. ALL WERE CHIPPED INTO SHAPE USING HAMMER STONES AND DEER ANTLERS.

PROJECTILE POINT STYLES CHANGED THROUGH TIME.

LARGE SIZE, DISTINCT SHOULDERS, STEMMED BASE.

SAVANNAH RIVER POINT
ABOUT 3000 TO 1000 B.C.

MORROW MOUNTAIN POINT
ABOUT 4000 TO 3000 B.C.

OVAL SHAPE, ROUNDED BASE, OFTEN MADE OF QUARTZ.

STANLY POINT
ABOUT 5000 TO 4000 B.C.

SLIGHT SHOULDERS, STEMMED BASE.

KIRK POINT
ABOUT 6000 TO 5000 B.C.

SERRATED (SAW-LIKE) BLADE EDGES, CORNER NOTCHES.

PALMER POINT
ABOUT 7000 TO 6000 B.C.

BEVELED BLADE EDGES, GROUND (RUBBED TO MAKE IT DULL) BASE, SIDE NOTCHES.

WOODLAND INDIAN PERIOD

1,000 B.C. TO A.D. 800

IN THE ARCHAIC INDIAN PERIOD, PEOPLE CLEARED THE FOREST MAINLY TO AID IN HUNTING. IN THE WOODLAND PERIOD, THE PRIMARY USE OF THESE CLEARINGS WAS FOR AGRICULTURE. WOODLAND PEOPLE HAD DISCOVERED THAT THE MOST FERTILE CLEARINGS WERE THOSE IN THE <u>FLOODPLAINS</u> (LOW LAND THAT IS FLOODED DURING TIMES OF HEAVY RAIN). THIS IS WHERE THEY DID THEIR GARDENING. WOMEN NOW SAVED THE SEEDS OF THEIR BEST PLANTS IN THE AUTUMN. THEN THEY PREPARED THE SOIL AND PLANTED THOSE SEEDS THE NEXT SPRING. THIS PROCESS OF SEED SELECTION BROUGHT ABOUT CHANGES IN THE PLANTS AND THE FRUITS THEY PRODUCED. SEEDS OF THE FATTEST, JUICIEST SQUASH, AND OF THE LARGEST SUNFLOWERS, WERE SELECTED.

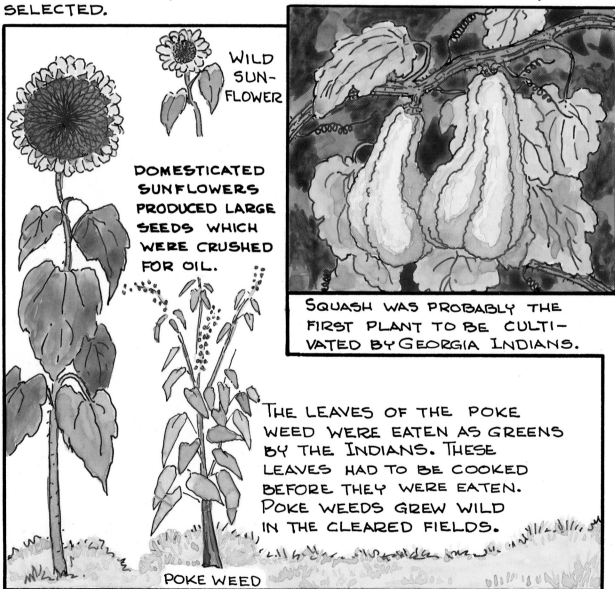

WILD SUN-FLOWER

DOMESTICATED SUNFLOWERS PRODUCED LARGE SEEDS WHICH WERE CRUSHED FOR OIL.

SQUASH WAS PROBABLY THE FIRST PLANT TO BE CULTI-VATED BY GEORGIA INDIANS.

THE LEAVES OF THE POKE WEED WERE EATEN AS GREENS BY THE INDIANS. THESE LEAVES HAD TO BE COOKED BEFORE THEY WERE EATEN. POKE WEEDS GREW WILD IN THE CLEARED FIELDS.

POKE WEED

With the addition of gardening, which provided a more dependable source of food, Woodland people were less nomadic than their Archaic Indian ancestors. Small villages, with well-made houses, were soon built near the seasonal gardens. People began to stay at these villages for longer and longer periods each year. Well over half their food still came from hunting, fishing, and gathering wild plants.

At sites of the Woodland Period, archaeologists find the earliest <u>POSTMOLDS</u> (stains in the soil caused by decayed logs used in construction). Woodland postmold patterns are circular, with a diameter of about 5 meters (roughly 16 feet). There is usually a large rock-lined fireplace at the center of each pattern. Woodland sites have a thick layer of archaeological remains. This suggests that these sites were occupied again and again over many years.

POST-MOLDS

FIRE PLACE

POSTMOLD PATTERN OF A CIRCULAR HOUSE OF THE WOODLAND PERIOD.

This is how a village of the Woodland Period may have looked. Walls of the houses were covered with cane mats or mud. The roofs were grass thatch or slabs of tree bark.

During the Woodland Period, populations increased steadily over most of Georgia. This increase came about because of the abundant food and the more settled existence provided by agriculture. People soon found a need for organizing their society in a different way. The new organization is called a "TRIBE."

Far back in the Archaic Period, those bands living close to one another had developed strong ties. A member of one band sometimes married someone from a neighboring band. This produced family ties. Strong links were also maintained through trade. By Woodland times, kinship and trade ties had become so strong between some bands that they came to think of themselves as one people.

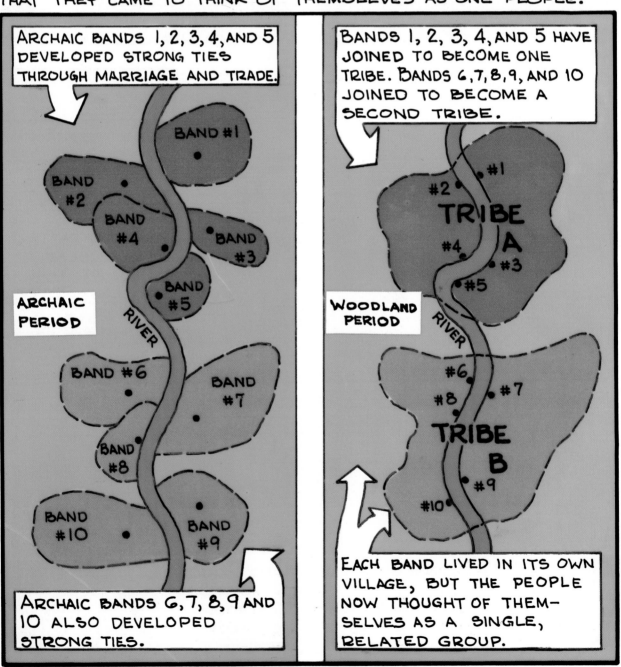

ARCHAIC BANDS 1, 2, 3, 4, AND 5 DEVELOPED STRONG TIES THROUGH MARRIAGE AND TRADE.

BAND #1

BAND #2

BAND #4

BAND #3

BAND #5

ARCHAIC PERIOD

RIVER

BAND #6

BAND #7

BAND #8

BAND #10

BAND #9

ARCHAIC BANDS 6, 7, 8, 9 AND 10 ALSO DEVELOPED STRONG TIES.

BANDS 1, 2, 3, 4, AND 5 HAVE JOINED TO BECOME ONE TRIBE. BANDS 6, 7, 8, 9, AND 10 JOINED TO BECOME A SECOND TRIBE.

#1

#2

TRIBE A

#4

#3

#5

WOODLAND PERIOD

RIVER

#6

#8

#7

TRIBE B

#9

#10

EACH BAND LIVED IN ITS OWN VILLAGE, BUT THE PEOPLE NOW THOUGHT OF THEM-SELVES AS A SINGLE, RELATED GROUP.

ARCHAIC SPEAR POINT

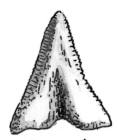

STONE ARROW POINTS

SHARK'S TOOTH ARROW POINT

DEER ANTLER ARROW POINT

EARLY IN THE WOODLAND PERIOD, THE BOW-AND-ARROW WAS DEVELOPED AS A NEW HUNTING WEAPON. EVIDENCE FOR THE BOW-AND-ARROW IS SEEN IN SMALLER PROJECTILE POINTS, SOME MADE OF STONE AND SOME OF OTHER MATERIALS.

WOODLAND ARROW POINTS

P-TUNG

ARCHAIC SPEAR POINTS WERE TOO HEAVY TO BE USED AS ARROW POINTS.

During the Woodland Period, the knowledge of pottery making spread to all the people in Georgia. In most groups, the potters were women. The pictures on this page show how this pottery was made.

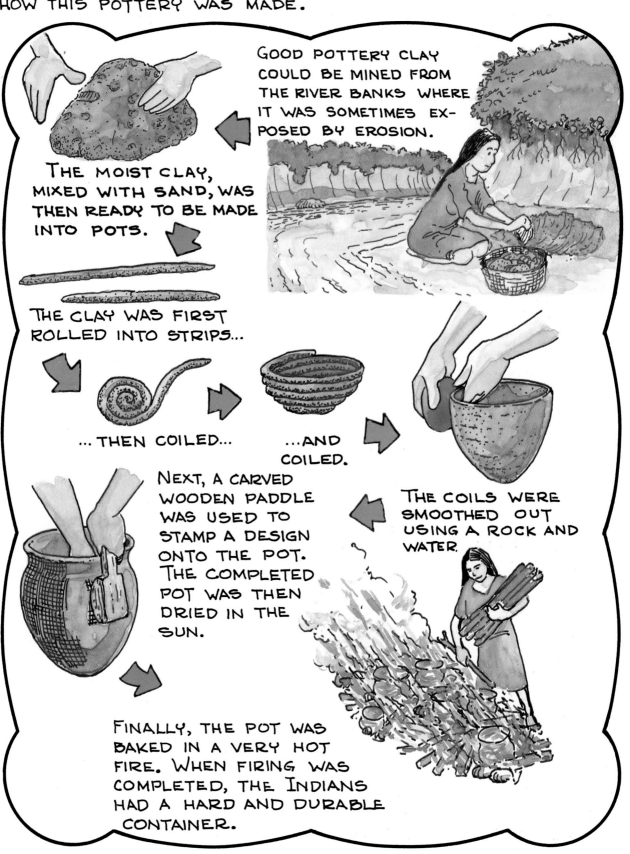

Good pottery clay could be mined from the river banks where it was sometimes exposed by erosion.

The moist clay, mixed with sand, was then ready to be made into pots.

The clay was first rolled into strips...

...then coiled...

...and coiled.

The coils were smoothed out using a rock and water.

Next, a carved wooden paddle was used to stamp a design onto the pot. The completed pot was then dried in the sun.

Finally, the pot was baked in a very hot fire. When firing was completed, the Indians had a hard and durable container.

GEORGIA INDIANS PREFERRED TO DECORATE THEIR POTTERY BY INCISING (SCRATCHING), IMPRESSING, OR STAMPING THE SURFACES. PAINTED POTTERY IS RARE IN GEORGIA. DESIGNS ON POTTERY CHANGED THROUGH THE CENTURIES. ARCHAEOLOGISTS STUDY THESE DESIGNS IN ORDER TO DETERMINE THE TIME PERIOD IN WHICH EACH WAS POPULAR. SHAPE CHANGED AS WELL. IN ADDITION, INDIAN POTTERS ADDED VARIOUS MATERIALS TO THE WET CLAY IN ORDER TO MAKE IT WORK PROPERLY. WE HAVE ALREADY NOTED THAT PLANT FIBERS WERE ADDED TO THE EARLIEST POTTERY. LATER, THEY MIXED SAND, CRUSHED QUARTZ, OR CRUSHED LIMESTONE WITH THE CLAY.

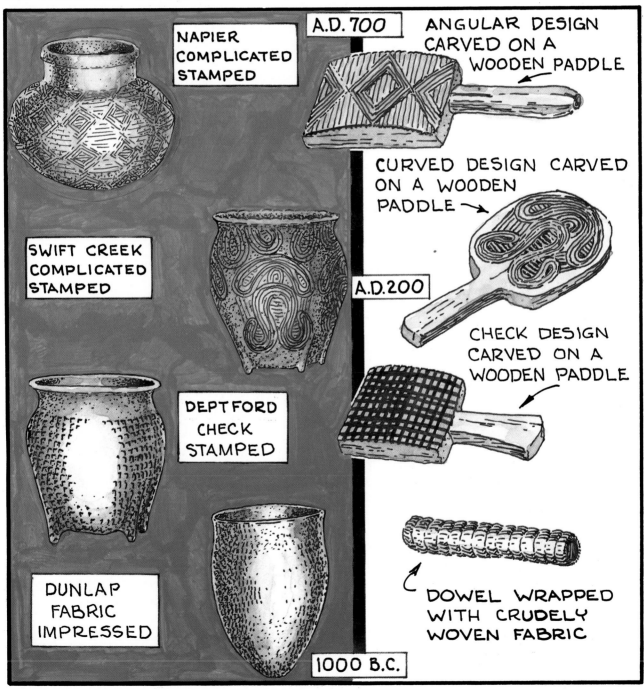

NAPIER COMPLICATED STAMPED

A.D. 700

ANGULAR DESIGN CARVED ON A WOODEN PADDLE

CURVED DESIGN CARVED ON A WOODEN PADDLE

SWIFT CREEK COMPLICATED STAMPED

A.D. 200

CHECK DESIGN CARVED ON A WOODEN PADDLE

DEPTFORD CHECK STAMPED

DUNLAP FABRIC IMPRESSED

DOWEL WRAPPED WITH CRUDELY WOVEN FABRIC

1000 B.C.

WOODLAND POTTERY TYPES IN GEORGIA

AFTER AGRICULTURE BECAME AN IMPORTANT SOURCE OF FOOD, PEOPLE COULD LIVE IN SMALLER TERRITORIES AND THEY COULD STAY MUCH OF THE YEAR IN ONE VILLAGE. ALSO, THERE WERE MANY CHANGES IN RELIGIOUS PRACTICES AND IN IDEAS ABOUT PEOPLE AND NATURE. SPECIAL PEOPLE, CALLED PRIESTS, WERE NECESSARY TO HELP WOODLAND INDIANS COMMUNICATE WITH SPIRITS AND TO LEAD RELIGIOUS CEREMONIES.

AGRICULTURE AND THE SPIRITS OF NATURE:

PLANTING:
PEOPLE OF THE WOODLAND PERIOD BELIEVED THAT SPIRITS WITHIN SEEDS HAD TO BE MADE HAPPY SO THAT THE SEEDS WOULD GROW INTO HEALTHY PLANTS. THE PRIEST LED PLANTING CEREMONIES IN THE SPRING.

CARING FOR THE CROPS:
TOO MUCH RAIN MIGHT WASH AWAY THE GARDENS. TOO LITTLE RAIN WOULD DRY UP THE CROPS. THE SUN COULD BURN YOUNG PLANTS, AND A COLD WIND COULD BLOW IN A LATE FREEZE AND KILL THE CROP. THIS MADE IT IMPORTANT TO CONDUCT CEREMONIES THAT WOULD PLEASE THE SPIRITS OF NATURE.

HARVESTING THE CROPS:
BY LATE SUMMER, CROPS WERE READY TO BE HARVESTED. THE SPIRITS AGAIN WERE THANKED SO THAT THEY WOULD COOPERATE DURING THE NEXT PLANTING AND GROWING SEASON.

FORT MOUNTAIN
IN
MURRAY COUNTY

WOODLAND TRIBES SET ASIDE SPECIAL AREAS FOR RELIGIOUS OBSERVANCES AND CEREMONIES. A CEREMONIAL SITE WAS A SYMBOL OF UNITY TO THE PEOPLE WHO USED IT. ONE SUCH SITE, IN MURRAY COUNTY, IS CALLED "FORT MOUNTAIN," BECAUSE IT LOOKED LIKE A MILITARY FORT TO EARLY EUROPEAN SETTLERS. HERE, A STONE WALL SURROUNDS THE SUMMIT OF A SMALL MOUNTAIN. IMPORTANT CEREMONIES WERE CONDUCTED WITHIN THIS ENCLOSURE AROUND A.D. 100 TO 400. ENCLOSURES SIMILAR TO FORT MOUNTAIN HAVE BEEN FOUND IN MANY PARTS OF THE EASTERN UNITED STATES. SOME OF THEM ARE BUILT OF EARTH, WHEREAS OTHERS ARE MADE OF STONE.

ANOTHER SITE OF THE WOODLAND PERIOD IS LOCATED IN PUTNAM COUNTY. IT IS CALLED THE "ROCK EAGLE MOUND". FROM ABOVE, THIS CONSTRUCTION LOOKS LIKE A LARGE BIRD, MAYBE AN EAGLE. SINCE FEW ARTIFACTS HAVE BEEN FOUND AT THIS SITE, ARCHAEOLOGISTS BELIEVE THAT IT WAS RESERVED FOR SPECIAL CEREMONIES, SIMILAR TO FORT MOUNTAIN. THE ROCK EAGLE MOUND WAS BUILT ABOUT A.D. 200.

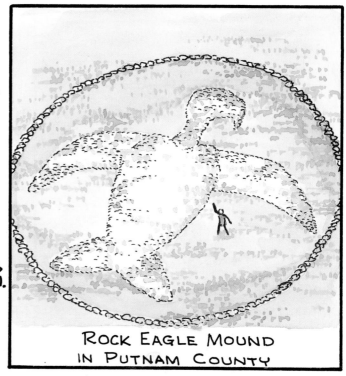

ROCK EAGLE MOUND
IN PUTNAM COUNTY

THE PRIESTS, WHO COULD TALK WITH THE SPIRITS, WERE TREATED WITH REVERENCE AND RESPECT. THESE PRIESTS LED THE CEREMONIES OF PLANTING AND HARVESTING. THEY CALLED ON THEIR PEOPLE TO BUILD CEREMONIAL STRUCTURES SUCH AS FORT MOUNTAIN AND ROCK EAGLE. WHEN A PRIEST DIED, IT WAS A VERY SORROWFUL EVENT. THE BODY OF THE PRIEST WAS USUALLY PLACED IN A SMALL EARTHEN OR STONE MOUND. SPECIAL OBJECTS, SUCH AS FLINT BLADES, POTTERY FIGURINES, AND STONE PIPES, WERE BURIED WITH THE BODY.

THE VALLEY OF THE OHIO RIVER SEEMS TO HAVE BEEN THE CENTER OF RELIGIOUS DEVELOPMENT IN THE WOODLAND PERIOD. FROM THERE,

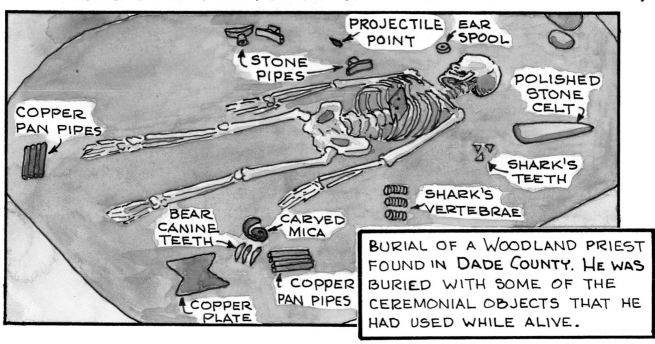

PROJECTILE POINT

EAR SPOOL

STONE PIPES

POLISHED STONE CELT

COPPER PAN PIPES

SHARK'S TEETH

SHARK'S VERTEBRAE

BEAR CANINE TEETH

CARVED MICA

COPPER PAN PIPES

COPPER PLATE

BURIAL OF A WOODLAND PRIEST FOUND IN DADE COUNTY. HE WAS BURIED WITH SOME OF THE CEREMONIAL OBJECTS THAT HE HAD USED WHILE ALIVE.

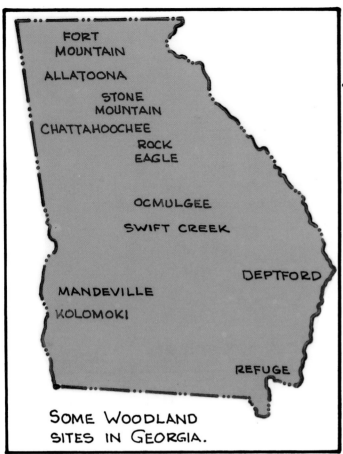

SOME WOODLAND
SITES IN GEORGIA.

IDEAS SPREAD OVER THE ENTIRE EASTERN WOODLANDS. THE CULTURE OF THE OHIO VALLEY DURING THE WOODLAND PERIOD IS CALLED "HOPEWELL" BY ARCHAEOLOGISTS. INFLUENCE OF THE HOPEWELL CULTURE IS FOUND AT SEVERAL SITES IN GEORGIA. THIS DOES NOT MEAN THAT PEOPLE OF THE OHIO VALLEY CAME TO GEORGIA TO LIVE. WHAT IT PROBABLY DOES MEAN IS THAT PRIESTS OF THE GEORGIA TRIBES BORROWED THE BELIEFS AND CEREMONIES OF HOPEWELL PRIESTS.

HOW DID HOPEWELL IDEAS SPREAD FROM THE OHIO VALLEY TO GEORGIA? ARCHAEOLOGISTS THINK THAT TRADE WAS THE REASON. PRIESTS OF THE HOPEWELL CULTURE USED SPECIAL MATERIALS FOR THEIR CEREMONIAL OBJECTS. FOR EXAMPLE, THEY USED OBSIDIAN (NATURAL GLASS) FROM THE ROCKY MOUNTAINS FOR CERE-MONIAL BLADES. THEY MADE OTHER SACRED OBJECTS FROM MICA, SHELLS, COPPER, ANIMAL BONES, AND FLINT. SINCE THESE MATERIALS COULD ONLY BE FOUND IN CERTAIN AREAS, THEY HAD TO BE OBTAINED BY TRADE FROM THE TRIBES THAT LIVED IN THOSE SOURCE AREAS. EVERYWHERE THE TRADERS WENT, THEY SPREAD HOPEWELL IDEAS ABOUT SPIRITS AND NATURE, AND ABOUT THE CEREMONIES OF THE PRIESTS.

THE WOODLAND PERIOD SAW THE SPREAD OF THE BOW-AND-ARROW, POTTERY, AND AGRICULTURE TO EVERY PART OF THE EASTERN FOREST. LIFE NOW CENTERED AROUND SMALL TRIBAL VILLAGES. THANKS TO THESE DEVELOPMENTS, POPULATION INCREASED GREATLY. WE FIND EVIDENCE OF THESE DYNAMIC PEOPLE ALL OVER GEORGIA.

INDIANS HAD KNOWN FOR THOUSANDS OF YEARS THAT SEEDS GREW INTO PLANTS, BUT WHEN WOODLAND INDIANS BEGAN TO SAVE SEEDS IN THE FALL SO THAT THEY COULD PLANT THEM THE NEXT SPRING THEY WERE PARTICIPATING IN ONE OF NATURE'S GREATEST MYS-TERIES. THE POWER OF THE PRIESTS GREW, AND AS IT GREW, IT COMPLETELY ALTERED WOODLAND CULTURE. THE "MISSISSIPPIAN" PERIOD CAME NEXT.

WOODLAND PERIOD ⟶ MISSISSIPPIAN PERIOD
1000 B.C.   A.D. 800   A.D. 1540

MISSISSIPPIAN INDIAN PERIOD
A.D. 800 TO A.D. 1540

BY A.D. 800, THE INDIANS OF GEORGIA WERE DEVELOPING A NEW WAY OF LIFE — A NEW CULTURE — WHICH ARCHAEOLOGISTS CALL "MISSISSIPPIAN." WE USE THE NAME MISSISSIPPIAN BECAUSE SOME OF THE FIRST SIGNS OF THIS NEW CULTURE HAVE BEEN FOUND AT VILLAGES ALONG THE MISSISSIPPI RIVER BETWEEN MODERN-DAY ST. LOUIS, MISSOURI AND MEMPHIS, TENNESSEE. GEORGIA HAS SOME VERY IMPORTANT SITES OF THE MISSISSIPPIAN PERIOD.

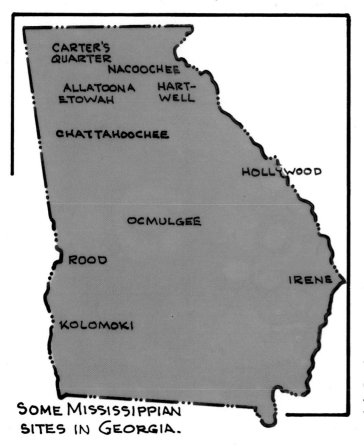

SOME MISSISSIPPIAN SITES IN GEORGIA.

PEOPLE OF THIS PERIOD, LIKE THEIR WOODLAND PERIOD ANCESTORS, BUILT VILLAGES ALONG THE MAJOR RIVERS. HOWEVER, VILLAGES OF THE MISSISSIPPIAN PERIOD WERE MUCH LARGER AND MORE PERMANENT THAN WOODLAND VILLAGES. ALL FARMING WAS DONE IN THE RIVER FLOODPLAINS, WHERE LARGE AREAS WERE CLEARED FOR CULTIVATION. SOMETIMES MISSISSIPPIAN PEOPLE HAD TO SHIFT THE LOCATIONS OF THE FIELDS FROM YEAR TO YEAR TO KEEP FROM USING UP THE NATURAL FERTILITY IN THE SOIL. THIS TYPE OF AGRICULTURE IS CALLED "SHIFTING AGRICULTURE."

Mississippian Indians grew many kinds of vegetables in the fields around their villages. They also hunted, fished, and collected wild plants in ways similar to their ancestors. Sometimes there would be an extra good year when much food was produced. During these years, the villagers would store some of the surplus food in community storehouses.

The most important cultivated plants in the Mississippian period were corn (maize), beans, squash, and pumpkins. Because of the abundant and reliable food from these plants, the people were able to live in large, permanent villages. How did the plants come to be <u>DOMESTICATED</u> (controlled by man) and what was their place of origin? Corn, beans, squash, and pumpkins all grew wild in Central Mexico between 8,000 and 4,000 B.C. Mexican Indians began to collect these wild plants for food. Over many generations, they learned to select and plant the better seeds. Through this

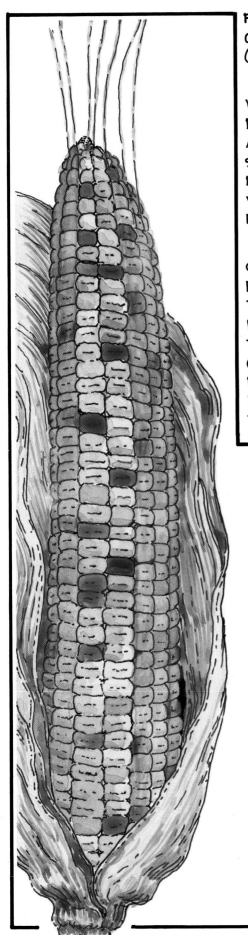

PROCESS, THE PLANTS WERE GRADUALLY CHANGED TO BE MORE <u>PRODUCTIVE</u> (LARGER AND EASIER TO GROW).

AS THE PLANTS WERE IMPROVED, THEY WERE ADOPTED BY INDIANS IN MANY PARTS OF NORTH AMERICA AND SOUTH AMERICA. BY THE TIME CORN REACHED SOUTHEASTERN INDIANS IN THE MISSISSIPPIAN PERIOD, IT HAD BECOME VERY DIFFERENT FROM ITS ORIGINAL FORM.

CORN, BEANS, SQUASH, AND PUMPKINS GREW WELL TOGETHER. THE CORN STALK PROVIDED A POLE FOR THE BEAN VINES TO CLIMB, THE CORN LEAVES MADE SHADE FOR THE SQUASH AND PUMPKINS, AND THE SQUASH AND PUMPKIN VINES CROWDED OUT MANY WEEDS. MISSISSIPPIAN PEOPLE PLANTED THESE FOUR PLANTS TOGETHER IN "HILLS," RATHER THAN SEPARATING THEM IN ROWS AS DO MODERN FARMERS.

THE LARGE EAR ON THE LEFT IS SOUTHERN DENT CORN, WHICH WAS GROWN BY MISSISSIPPIAN PEOPLE IN GEORGIA. IT IS CALLED "DENT" CORN BECAUSE OF THE SLIGHT DENT FOUND IN MOST OF THE KERNELS. THE SMALL EAR ON THE RIGHT IS THE WILD ANCESTOR OF MODERN CORN. IT GREW IN CENTRAL MEXICO ABOUT 4,000 B.C. THIS WILD VARIETY IS NOW EXTINCT, BUT WE KNOW WHAT IT LOOKED LIKE BECAUSE EXAMPLES HAVE BEEN FOUND BY ARCHAEOLOGISTS IN DRY CAVE SITES IN MEXICO. BOTH EARS ARE SHOWN ACTUAL SIZE.

The settled and abundant life of the Mississippian period led to the development of a new type of society called a "Chiefdom." Chiefdoms are found in the world today in places such as Africa and the South Pacific Islands. In a chiefdom, families are RANKED (given a level of importance) according to how closely they are related to the ruling family. At the head of the ruling family was a powerful priest-chief. The position of priest-chief was inherited much like the kings of Europe. When the priest-chief died, his position was inherited by his sister's son, not his own son. This was because Mississippian people traced their family trees through the women rather than through the men as we do. Women also controlled the property of each family.

The priest-chief was well cared for by his family. He was dressed, fed, and carried wherever he went on a LITTER (a seat carried on poles). Some of his relatives also were priests and they assisted the priest-chief in important meetings and ceremonies.

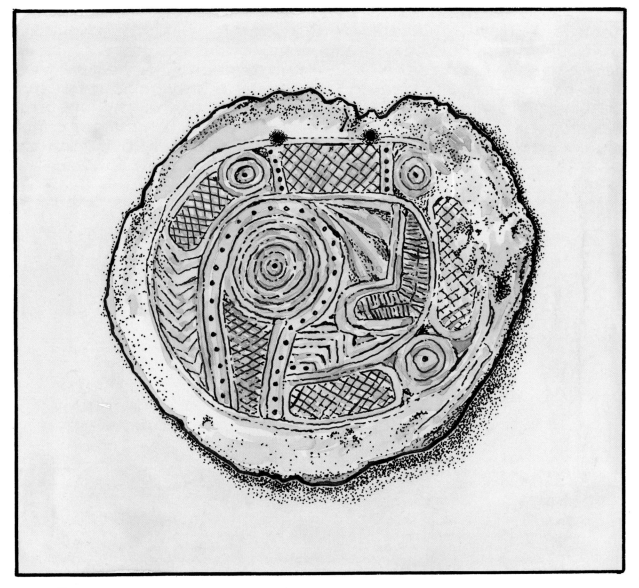

THE ARTIFACT SHOWN ABOVE IS CALLED A "GORGET" (PRONOUNCED GOR-JET). IT IS MADE FROM A PIECE OF CONCH SHELL, A KIND OF OCEAN SHELL THAT WAS HIGHLY VALUED BY MISSISSIPPIAN PEOPLE. THESE SHELLS WERE TRADED OVER LONG DISTANCES. THIS GORGET WAS CARVED AT THE LITTLE EGYPT SITE IN MURRAY COUNTY ABOUT A.D. 1500. IT WAS WORN BY THE PRIEST-CHIEF SHOWN ON THE OPPOSITE PAGE. THE DESIGN IS A COILED RATTLE-SNAKE WITH AN EAGLE'S EYE. CAN YOU FIND THE MOUTH, EYE, SCALES, AND RATTLES OF THE SNAKE?

THE DESIGNS ON SOME MISSISSIPPIAN ARTIFACTS ARE SIMILAR TO DESIGNS FOUND ON ARTIFACTS IN MEXICO. SOME ARCHAEOLO-GISTS THINK THAT MISSISSIPPIAN INDIANS AND THOSE IN MEXICO EXCHANGED RELIGIOUS IDEAS. POSSIBLY THERE WAS CONTACT DURING LONG-DISTANCE TRADING EXPEDITIONS. ANOTHER POSSIBILITY IS THAT THE IDEAS WERE TRANSFERRED BY INTERMEDIATE GROUPS, WITHOUT DIRECT CONTACT BY PEOPLE FROM THE TWO AREAS.

Indians of the Mississippian Period did not leave written records, but they left many elaborate objects that tell us about their culture. Their ceremonial objects were made from stone, wood, seashells, and copper. The artifact below is an embossed copper plate showing a dancer in an eagle costume. This plate was hammered into shape and the design was put on with wooden or bone tools. Like most copper ornaments, it was made in several pieces and then riveted together. It was found at the Etowah site in Bartow County.

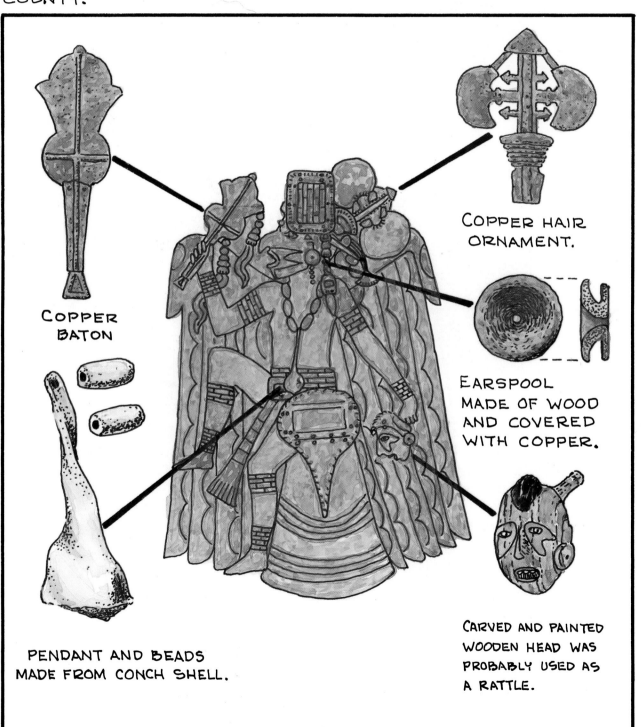

Copper Baton

Copper Hair Ornament.

Earspool made of wood and covered with copper.

Pendant and beads made from conch shell.

Carved and painted wooden head was probably used as a rattle.

THE PRIEST-CHIEF WAS THOUGHT BY HIS PEOPLE TO HAVE THE ABILITY TO TALK TO THE SPIRITS OF NATURE AND TO INFLUENCE THESE SPIRITS. PEOPLE EVEN THOUGHT OF THE PRIEST-CHIEF AS BEING RELATED TO CERTAIN ANIMAL SPIRITS. IN CEREMONIES, THE PRIEST-CHIEF AND HIS ASSISTANTS WOULD DRESS IN ANIMAL COSTUMES SO THAT THEY WOULD APPEAR AS HALF MEN AND HALF BEASTS. THE PRIEST-CHIEF ALWAYS ASKED THE SPIRITS TO GIVE HIS PEOPLE A GOOD HARVEST.

INDIANS OF THE MISSISSIPPIAN PERIOD MADE USE OF MANY PLANTS FOR PURPOSES OTHER THAN FOOD. TWO OF THESE PLANTS WERE WILD TOBACCO (<u>NICOTIANA RUSTICA</u>) AND YAUPON HOLLY (<u>ILEX VOMITORIA</u>). LEAVES OF THE TOBACCO PLANT WERE MIXED WITH VARIOUS OTHER PLANTS AND SMOKED IN PIPES OF CLAY AND STONE. LEAVES OF THE YAUPON HOLLY WERE DRIED AND BOILED TO MAKE A STRONG TEA, CALLED "BLACK DRINK." WHEN SWALLOWED IN LARGE AMOUNTS, BLACK DRINK CAUSED VOMITING. A FRENCHMAN, LOUIS MILFORT, LIVED WITH THE CREEK INDIANS FROM 1775 TO 1795. IN HIS BOOK, HE SAID: "They have the habit, before entering into any matter of beginning by smoking their pipe, and by taking drink which they make from the leaves of a tree which is very common in their country, and which is claimed to be a wild tea tree. It has been seen that Indians threw up this drink with a great deal of ease. The purpose of this disgusting ceremony is to assure the chief of the assembly that each of the members who compose it has a stomach free of food and consequently a clear head."

CLAY PIPES FOUND IN CHEROKEE COUNTY.

THERE WERE MANY SECRET CEREMONIES IN MISSISSIPPIAN SOCIETY. AT SOME VILLAGES, THESE CEREMONIES WERE HELD IN DIRT-COVERED BUILDINGS CALLED "EARTHLODGES." ONE VERY IMPORTANT CEREMONY WAS CALLED THE "BUSK." THE BUSK WAS OBSERVED EVERY SUMMER WHEN THE CORN WAS RIPENING. EARS OF THIS GREEN CORN WERE USED TO LIGHT A SACRED FIRE IN THE EARTHLODGE. THIS SYMBOLIZED THE BEGINNING OF A NEW YEAR.

TO THE RIGHT IS SHOWN THE RECONSTRUCTED EARTHLODGE AT OCMULGEE NATIONAL MONUMENT IN MACON, BIBB COUNTY. A CHARRED ROOF BEAM FROM THE RUINS OF THIS BUILDING HAS BEEN DATED BY THE RADIOCARBON TECHNIQUE AT A.D. 1050.

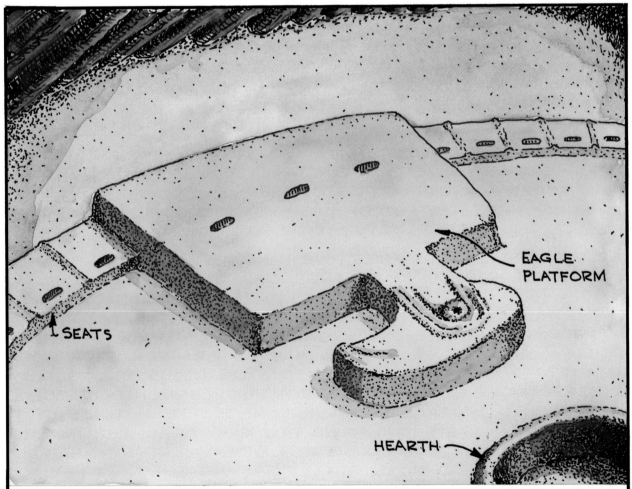

EAGLE PLATFORM

SEATS

HEARTH

INSIDE THE EARTHLODGE THERE WAS ROOM TO SEAT 47 NOBLES. THE PRIEST-CHIEF AND TWO OF HIS ASSISTANTS SAT ON A RAISED PLATFORM MADE IN THE SHAPE OF A BIRD.

SOME MISSISSIPPIAN VILLAGES WERE LARGER AND MORE POWER-
FUL THAN OTHERS. THESE ARE CALLED "CEREMONIAL CENTERS."
THE PRIEST-CHIEF AND HIS NOBLE FAMILY LIVED AT THE CERE-
MONIAL CENTER, AND THEY RULED AN AREA THAT MIGHT
INCLUDE SEVERAL HUNDRED SQUARE KILOMETERS. EACH OF THESE
CEREMONIAL CENTERS HAD ONE OR MORE LARGE, FLAT-TOPPED
EARTH MOUNDS. MISSISSIPPIAN MOUNDS SERVED AS PLATFORMS
FOR IMPORTANT BUILDINGS, SUCH AS THE HOUSES OF THE PRIEST-
CHIEF AND HIS FAMILY, BUILDINGS FOR RELIGIOUS AND POLITICAL
ACTIVITIES (TEMPLES), AND BUILDINGS WHERE THE REMAINS OF
THE NOBILITY WERE BURIED (MORTUARY HOUSES). SOME OF THE
LARGEST TEMPLE MOUNDS IN NORTH AMERICA ARE LOCATED AT
THE ETOWAH SITE IN BARTOW COUNTY, THE OCMULGEE SITE
IN BIBB COUNTY, AND THE KOLOMOKI SITE IN EARLY COUNTY.

THE DRAWING ON THE OPPOSITE PAGE SHOWS HOW ARCHAEOLO-
GISTS THINK THE ETOWAH SITE LOOKED ABOUT A.D. 1200-1500.
ETOWAH, LIKE MOST MISSISSIPPIAN VILLAGES, WAS SURROUNDED BY A
PALISADE (A WALL BUILT OF LARGE POSTS). IN ADDITION, THERE
WAS A WIDE DITCH JUST OUTSIDE THE PALISADE. THE DITCHES
AND PALISADES WERE CONSTRUCTED TO PROTECT THE
VILLAGERS AND THEIR STORE HOUSES OF FOOD FROM NEIGHBORING,
HOSTILE GROUPS. THE PALISADE STOOD BETWEEN 4 AND 6 METERS
HIGH (ABOUT 14 TO 20 FEET). BASTIONS (GUARD TOWERS) WERE
PLACED AT 30-METER (ABOUT 100 FEET) INTERVALS ALL AROUND
THE PALISADE.

VILLAGERS LIVED BOTH INSIDE AND OUTSIDE THE PALISADE.
THE CREEKS AND RIVERS OF THE AREA WERE THEIR HIGHWAYS.
THEIR STURDY CANOES CARRIED FISHERMEN, TRADERS AND
WARRIORS GREAT DISTANCES. THE BROAD FLOODPLAIN ON BOTH
SIDES OF THE RIVER PROVIDED RICH SOIL FOR AGRICULTURE.

OCCASIONALLY, THE PRIEST-CHIEF AND HIS ASSISTANTS WOULD
CALL ON THE PEOPLE TO ENLARGE ONE OF THE MOUNDS,
BUILD A NEW TEMPLE, OR STRENGTHEN THE PALISADE. THE
PEOPLE ALSO WORKED TOGETHER IN COMMUNITY GARDENS.
FOOD FROM THE COMMUNITY GARDENS WAS USED BY THE
NOBILITY SINCE THESE NOBLES HAD TO BE FREE FROM WORK
IN ORDER TO SPEND THEIR TIME ON RELIGIOUS AND POLITICAL
MATTERS. SOME OF THE FOOD FROM THE COMMUNITY GARDENS
WAS PUT INTO STORAGE FOR EVERYONE'S USE IN TIMES OF
NEED. ARCHAEOLOGISTS HAVE FOUND THAT MANY OF THE CEREMONIAL
CENTERS WERE LOCATED CLOSE TO A WIDE VARIETY OF NATURAL
RESOURCES, SUCH AS NUTS, SHELLFISH, AND FLINT. IT IS
POSSIBLE THAT THE PRIEST-CHIEF WAS RESPONSIBLE FOR
DISTRIBUTING THESE RESOURCES TO OUTLYING VILLAGES.

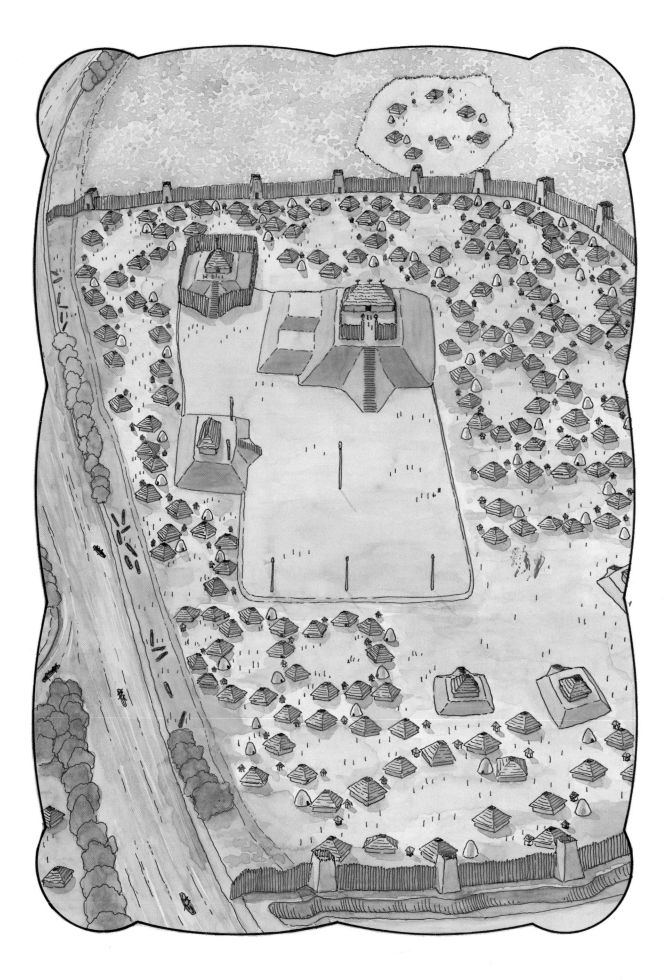

IN THEIR DAILY LIVES, THE AVERAGE CITIZENS OF MISSISSIPPIAN CULTURE WERE SELDOM CONCERNED WITH THE ACTIVITIES OF THE NOBILITY. THEY WERE BUSY HUNTING, COLLECTING EDIBLE NUTS, FISHING, AND CARING FOR THEIR GARDENS. THEY MADE POTTERY FROM LOCAL CLAYS AND DUG-OUT CANOES FROM THE TRUNKS OF LARGE TREES. THEY WOVE CLOTH AND REPAIRED THEIR HOUSES. THEY LAUGHED AT THE OLD PEOPLE'S STORIES, PLAYED BALL GAMES, AND MOURNED THE DEATHS OF RELATIVES. YOUNG MEN ASPIRED TO BE GOOD HUNTERS AND <u>ORATORS</u> (STORY TELLERS). YOUNG WOMEN HOPED TO BECOME SKILLED POTTERS AND TO MAKE WISE DECISIONS FOR THEIR FAMILIES. EVERYONE PRAYED THAT THE SPIRITS OF RAIN, WIND, AND SUN WOULD BE KIND.

IN THE MISSISSIPPIAN PERIOD, POTTERY WAS MADE IN A VARIETY OF SHAPES, SIZES, AND WITH MANY KINDS OF DECORATION. SOME POTS WERE FOR EVERYDAY USE, AND OTHERS WERE RESERVED FOR SPECIAL OCCASIONS.

THIS WATER BOTTLE, MADE IN THE SHAPE OF A DOG, WAS FOUND NEAR COLUMBUS IN MUSCOGEE COUNTY. IT DEMONSTRATES THE ARTISTIC SKILL ACHIEVED BY MISSISSIPPIAN POTTERS.

SMALL, DELICATE ARROW POINTS WERE MADE FROM STONE, WOOD, CANE, AND DEER ANTLERS. A COMMON MISTAKE IS TO CALL THEM "BIRD POINTS." ACTUALLY, <u>ALL</u> MISSISSIPPIAN ARROW POINTS WERE SMALL.

GAMES WERE VERY IMPORTANT IN MISSISSIPPIAN LIFE. THE GAME SHOWN HERE IS "CHUNKEY," WHICH WAS PLAYED WITH A LARGE STONE DISC AND WOODEN SPEARS. A PLAYER TRIED TO TOSS HIS SPEAR CLOSE TO WHERE HE THOUGHT THE DISC WOULD STOP ROLLING.

PEOPLE DECORATED THEMSELVES IN MANY WAYS. THEY USED BEADS, TATTOOING, PAINT, ELABORATE HAIRDOS, FEATHERS, AND MANY TYPES OF EAR ORNAMENTS.

LARGE TREES WERE CUT AND HOLLOWED OUT TO MAKE STURDY CANOES. THIS WORK WAS DONE WITH STONE TOOLS. THE MAN IS USING AN "ADZE."

YOU CAN EASILY SEE THAT THE INDIANS OF THE MISSISSIPPIAN PERIOD HAD A COMPLEX SOCIETY, POPULOUS SETTLEMENTS, AND A PRODUCTIVE ECONOMY. THIS CULTURE WAS THE PRODUCT OF 12,000 YEARS OF HUMAN DEVELOPMENT IN GEORGIA AND THE REST OF EASTERN NORTH AMERICA. WHEN EUROPEAN EXPLORERS FIRST CAME INTO SOUTHEASTERN NORTH AMERICA IN THE 1500'S, THEY FOUND THE MISSISSIPPIAN PEOPLE LIVING A PROSPEROUS LIFE.

HISTORIC PERIOD
A.D. 1540 TO PRESENT

THE HISTORIC PERIOD BEGAN IN GEORGIA WITH SPANISH EXPEDITIONS DURING THE 1500'S. THESE EXPEDITIONS USUALLY HAD A <u>CHRONICLER</u> (A PERSON WHO KEPT A LOG BOOK). IT WAS THE CHRONICLER'S DUTY TO NOTE INTERESTING FACTS ABOUT THE PEOPLE, ANIMALS, PLANTS, AND GEOGRAPHICAL FEATURES THAT THE EXPEDITION ENCOUNTERED. ALSO, HE KEPT A RECORD OF THE DISTANCE AND DIRECTION TRAVELED. SOME OF THESE WRITINGS HAVE BEEN PRESERVED UP TO THE PRESENT TIME. UNFORTUNATELY, HOWEVER, MOST CHRONICLERS LOOKED UPON THE INDIANS AS INFERIOR "SAVAGES." AS A RESULT, MANY OF THE DESCRIPTIONS OF THE INDIANS ARE BRIEF AND UNCLEAR.

THE FIRST EUROPEAN EXPLORERS TO REACH THE NEW WORLD WERE VIKINGS FROM NORWAY. THEY ESTABLISHED SMALL SETTLEMENTS ON THE COAST OF NORTH AMERICA AS EARLY AS A.D. 1000.

EVEN THOUGH HISTORIC DOCUMENTS ARE HELPFUL TO THE ARCHAEOLOGIST, HE MUST STILL RECOVER MATERIAL REMAINS IN ORDER TO GAIN A COMPLETE PICTURE OF THE CULTURES IN THE HISTORIC PERIOD. EVERY ARCHAEOLOGICAL PROJECT ON HISTORIC SITES REVEALS FACTS THAT ARE NOT FOUND IN THE WRITTEN RECORDS.

HERNANDO DESOTO WAS THE FIRST EUROPEAN EXPLORER TO VISIT THE AREA NOW CALLED GEORGIA. DESOTO AND HIS MEN SAILED FROM CUBA IN 1539. IN 1540, THEY MADE THEIR WAY INTO SOUTHEASTERN GEORGIA.

WITH DESOTO WERE 620 SOLDIERS

CALLED <u>CONQUISTADORES</u> (SPANISH FOR CONQUERORS), 8 PRIESTS, A LARGE NUMBER OF SLAVES, 200 HORSES, 300 FOOD ANIMALS, AND SEVERAL DOZEN HUGE DOGS TRAINED FOR BATTLE. DESOTO AND HIS MEN DREAMED OF FINDING GREAT WEALTH LIKE THE CONQUISTADORES HAD FOUND IN MEXICO AND PERU.

FROM SOUTH GEORGIA, DESOTO'S ARMY CROSSED THE SAVANNAH RIVER INTO SOUTH CAROLINA. FROM THERE, THEY MARCHED NORTH TO THE APPALACHIAN MOUNTAINS, AND THEN WEST TO ALABAMA AND MISSISSIPPI. ALTHOUGH DESOTO DIED IN 1542, HIS CONQUISTADORES CONTINUED THEIR EXPLORATIONS INTO AREAS WEST OF THE MISSISSIPPI RIVER BEFORE MAKING THEIR WAY BACK TO THE GULF OF MEXICO.

AS THE ARMY TRAVELED FROM VILLAGE TO VILLAGE, THE SOLDIERS SOMETIMES MISTREATED THE INDIANS. THEY OFTEN WOULD TAKE OVER ALL OF THE FOOD SUPPLY OF A VILLAGE, AND THEIR HORSES MIGHT EAT AN ENTIRE YEAR'S SUPPLY OF CORN IN A FEW DAYS. SOMETIMES THE SPANIARDS HELD A PRIEST-CHIEF HOSTAGE TO INSURE THE ARMY'S SAFE PASSAGE WITHIN HIS TERRITORY. IN THREE YEARS OF EXPLORATIONS IN THE SOUTHEAST, DESOTO FOUGHT NUMEROUS BATTLES WITH THE INDIANS, BUT HE FOUND NO GOLD OR OTHER VALUABLES.

MORE EUROPEAN EXPLORERS FOLLOWED DESOTO. THERE WERE MANY BATTLES, AND THOUSANDS OF INDIANS DIED. IN ADDITION, THE SPANISH BROUGHT EUROPEAN DISEASES SUCH AS MEASLES AND SMALL POX. THE INDIANS HAD NO IMMUNITY TO THESE DISEASES, AND THOUSANDS MORE DIED. WITH SO MUCH LOSS OF LIFE, MISSISSIPPIAN CULTURE COLLAPSED IN A FEW GENERATIONS. TREES GREW UP ON THE TEMPLE MOUNDS, AND THE MIGHTY CEREMONIES TO THE SUN, RAIN, AND WIND WERE ALL BUT FORGOTTEN. THESE CHANGES BROUGHT THE DEVELOPMENT OF HISTORIC INDIAN "NATIONS," SUCH AS THE CREEK, YUCHI, AND CHEROKEE. THESE TRIBES WERE REMNANTS OF THE EARLIER CHIEFDOMS.

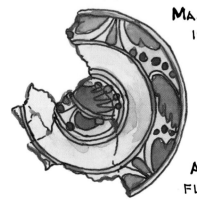

MAJOLICA POTTERY IS FOUND ON MANY SPANISH SITES FROM A.D. 1600 TO 1700. THIS PLATE WAS FOUND AT ST. AUGUSTINE, FLORIDA.

INDIANS VALUED EUROPEAN IRON TOOLS. THIS SMALL IRON AXE HEAD WAS FOUND AT A VILLAGE SITE IN FLOYD COUNTY.

BY 1600, THREE EURO-
PEAN POWERS—ENGLAND, SPAIN,
AND FRANCE—HAD LAID CLAIM
TO PARTS OF THE SOUTHEAST.
REPRESENTATIVES OF THESE
THREE COUNTRIES COMPETED
FOR THE FRIENDSHIP OF THE
INDIANS. ONE COUNTRY WOULD
OFFER A GROUP OF INDIANS
GUNS AND OTHER TRADE GOODS
IN EXCHANGE FOR THE INDIANS'
HELP IN PROTECTING THAT
COUNTRY'S LAND CLAIMS. THE
INDIANS DID NOT REALIZE
THAT THE FRIENDSHIP WAS
NOT GENUINE AND THAT THEY
WERE ONLY BEING USED.

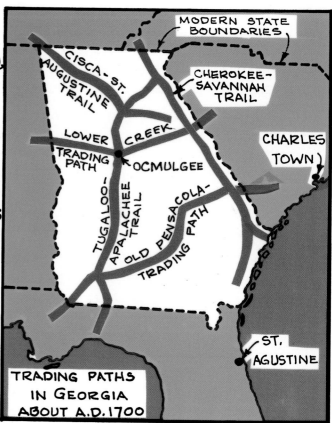

TRADING PATHS
IN GEORGIA
ABOUT A.D. 1700

BY THE LATE 1600'S THE
ENGLISH HAD BECOME THE DOM-
INANT POWER IN THE SOUTHEAST
AND HAD ESTABLISHED REGULAR TRADE RELATIONS WITH THE
INDIANS IN GEORGIA. MOST OF THESE TRADERS WERE BASED
IN CHARLES TOWNE (CHARLESTON, SOUTH CAROLINA). THESE TRADERS
BROUGHT GUNS, AMMUNITION, GLASS BEADS, BRASS BELLS, METAL
HATCHETS, CLOTH, AND WHISKEY. FOR THESE GOODS, THE INDIANS
EXCHANGED DEER HIDES AND THE PELTS OF SMALL FUR-BEARING
ANIMALS.

GEORGIA INDIANS RAPIDLY BECAME DEPENDENT ON THE
TRADERS FOR SURVIVAL. FOR EXAMPLE, A FAMILY WITH ONLY

THE OCMULGEE TRADING POST
ABOUT 1710

BOWS AND ARROWS COULD NOT COMPETE IN WARFARE OR HUNTING WITH NEIGHBORS ARMED WITH ENGLISH GUNS. AS THE DEPENDENCE ON TRADE INCREASED, INDIAN MEN SPENT MORE AND MORE TIME AWAY FROM HOME ON HUNTING EXPEDITIONS. BY 1750, THERE WERE FEW DEER LEFT TO BE HUNTED.

BRASS TRADE BELL FOUND AT OCMULGEE

SOME OF THE TRADERS WERE DISHONEST IN THEIR DEALINGS WITH THE INDIANS. FROM TIME TO TIME, THIS DISHONESTY WOULD CAUSE THE INDIANS TO REBEL. WHEN A REBELLION DEVELOPED, THE ENGLISH WOULD HAVE A "TALK" WITH THE INDIANS TO TRY TO REGAIN THEIR COOPERATION. IN ONE SUCH TALK, GOVERNOR GLEN TOLD THE INDIANS: *"I shall conclude with an advice to such of your warriours as are too young to remember when you first had a trade with the English. Let them consult your old men, what was the condition of your country at that time, and compare it with your circumstances now. Instead of the admirable fire arms that you are now plentifully supplied with, your best arms were bad bows, and wretched arrows headed with bills of birds, bones of fishes, or at best with sharp stones. Instead of being decently or comfortable dressed in English cloaths, you were forced to cover yourselves with the skins of wild beasts. Your knives were split canes, and your hatchets were of stone..."*

IN 1690, SEVERAL GROUPS OF CREEK INDIANS MOVED THEIR TOWNS FROM THE CHATTAHOOCHEE RIVER TO THE OCMULGEE RIVER NEAR MODERN-DAY MACON. THE ENGLISH BUILT A TRADING POST THERE AND IT CONTINUED IN USE UNTIL 1715 WHEN THE YAMASSEE WAR BROKE OUT. OF THE 100 TRADERS LIVING AMONG THE CREEKS, 90 WERE KILLED IN THE FIRST FEW DAYS OF THIS WAR. CHARLES TOWNE ITSELF WAS IN GRAVE DANGER OF BEING ATTACKED BY THE INDIANS. BUT THE CREEKS LOST THE WAR AND THEY MOVED THEIR TOWNS BACK TO THE CHATTAHOOCHEE.

FORT FREDERICA IN 1736

THE COLONY OF GEORGIA WAS OFFICIALLY ESTABLISHED IN 1733 BY JAMES OGLETHORPE. SAVANNAH WAS THE FIRST SETTLEMENT. SOUTH OF SAVANNAH LAY SPANISH FLORIDA WITH ITS LARGE SETTLEMENT AT ST. AUGUSTINE. OGLETHORPE FEARED THAT THE SPANISH MIGHT ATTACK HIS NEW COLONY, AND IN 1736 HE BUILT SEVERAL FORTS TO PROTECT HIS SOUTHERN BOUNDARY. ONE OF THESE WAS FORT FREDERICA ON ST. SIMON'S ISLAND. IN 1739, THE WAR OF JENKIN'S EAR BEGAN BETWEEN SPAIN AND ENGLAND. FORT FREDERICA WAS USED BY OGLETHORPE TO LAUNCH RAIDS INTO FLORIDA. THE FORT ITSELF WAS ATTACKED BY SPANISH TROOPS IN 1742. FORT FREDERICA WAS ABANDONED AFTER THE TREATY BETWEEN ENGLAND AND SPAIN IN 1748.

**MODERN DAY VIEW
FROM FORT FREDERICA**

THE SOLDIERS AT FORT FREDERICA WORKED HARD CLEARING LAND AND KEEPING THE FORT IN REPAIR. AFTER A LONG DAY, THERE WAS TIME FOR RELAXATION. IN 1738, OGLETHORPE REPORTED THAT *"the people have been healthy."*

STONEWARE MUG FROM TOWN SITE

IRON AXE HEAD FROM FORT SITE

As the colony of Georgia grew, its new citizens pushed inland, settling first in the coastal plain, and then in the Piedmont and Mountains. Sometimes these settlers claimed land that belonged to the Indians, and conflict resulted. War between the colonies and England also was brewing, which resulted in the Revolutionary War of 1776-1783.

During the Revolutionary War, many of the Indians sided with England. After the war, the new state of Georgia began taking away the remaining lands of the Indians. To try to protect Indian rights and property, the United States Government sent an "Indian Agent" to the Southeast. This agent was Benjamin Hawkins. Hawkins set up his agency near present-day Thomaston. He proposed to "civilize" the Creek Indians by teaching them to raise cattle, to weave on a loom, and to do carpentry and metalwork in the European style.

Benjamin Hawkins
Agent to the Southern
Indians from A.D. 1798
to 1815.

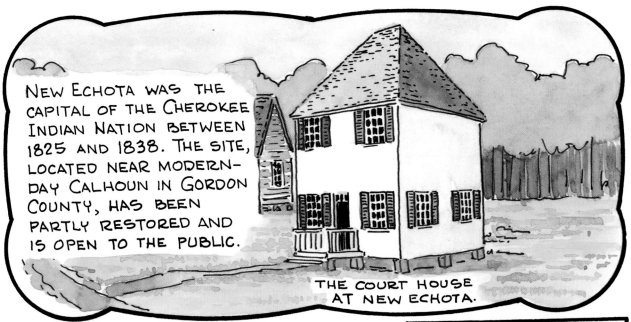

NEW ECHOTA WAS THE CAPITAL OF THE CHEROKEE INDIAN NATION BETWEEN 1825 AND 1838. THE SITE, LOCATED NEAR MODERN-DAY CALHOUN IN GORDON COUNTY, HAS BEEN PARTLY RESTORED AND IS OPEN TO THE PUBLIC.

THE COURT HOUSE AT NEW ECHOTA.

BY THE EARLY 1830's CHEROKEE INDIANS IN NORTHERN GEORGIA HAD ACCEPTED MANY OF THE WAYS OF THE "WHITE MEN," WHO WERE MOVING ONTO INDIAN LANDS IN EVER-INCREASING NUMBERS. THE CHEROKEES DREW UP A CONSTITUTION AND ESTABLISHED A CENTRAL GOVERNMENT, ALL PATTERNED AFTER THE UNITED STATES GOVERNMENT. HEADQUARTERS FOR THEIR GOVERNMENT, AS WELL AS A PRESS FOR PUBLISHING THEIR OWN NEWSPAPER, THE <u>CHEROKEE PHOENIX</u>, WAS LOCATED AT NEW ECHOTA, IN GORDON COUNTY.

IN THE 1830's, A LAW WAS PASSED BY THE UNITED STATES GOVERNMENT THAT RE-QUIRED THE INDIANS TO MOVE TO LANDS WEST OF THE MISSISSIPPI RIVER. THUS, ALL OF THE EFFORTS OF GEORGIA'S INDIANS TO ADAPT TO THE WAYS AND NEEDS OF A FOREIGN CULTURE HAD FAILED. SOME CHEROKEES, WHO DID NOT LEAVE GEORGIA VOLUNTARILY, WERE ROUNDED UP BY FEDERAL TROOPS AND FORCED TO MAKE THE LONG WESTWARD TRIP IN THE WINTER. MANY DIED BECAUSE OF INADEQUATE FOOD AND CLOTHING. THE CHEROKEES REMEMBER THIS TRAGIC JOURNEY AS THE "TRAIL OF TEARS."

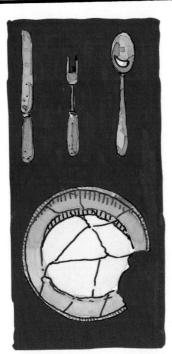

EUROPEAN-MADE EATING UTENSILS FROM NEW ECHOTA. A.D. 1825-1838

ALTHOUGH FEW INDIANS WERE LEFT IN GEORGIA AFTER 1840, A LEGACY OF THEIR RICH CULTURE REMAINED. CORN, BEANS, SQUASH, PUMPKINS, AND TOBACCO WERE INDIAN PLANTS. SETTLERS BUILT THEIR CABINS USING NATIVE CONSTRUCTION TECHNIQUES. EVEN TODAY WE USE MEDICINES INVENTED BY NATIVE AMERICANS.

By the early 1800's, an industrialized culture was developing in many parts of Georgia. Railroads, factories, and cities began to replace the footpaths, trading posts, and villages of earlier times. In some areas, agriculture was practiced on large plantations, where cotton, rice, and sugar cane were important crops. Blacks were imported from Africa to be used as labor on many plantations.

Archaeologists have excavated plantation sites on Georgia's coastal islands. Artifacts from the houses of the plantation owners have been compared with those from the houses of the overseers and the slaves. From these studies, we are learning about many facets of life on a nineteenth-century plantation.

At the Civil War battle site of Pickett's Mill in Paulding County, archaeologists have excavated the remains of a small farm house that was present during the fighting. As the armies came closer, Zach Brand and his family had to evacuate their home. The house was severely damaged during the battle.

Disputes between the northern and southern states, especially a growing distaste in the north for slavery, led to the outbreak of the American Civil War in 1861. Toward the end of the war, in 1864, an important military campaign was fought along a route between Dalton and Atlanta. After several severe battles around Atlanta, in which the Confederate Army was defeated, the Federal Army marched on to Savannah. The Atlanta Campaign and the "March to the Sea," left many of Georgia's towns, farms, and plantations in ruin.

After the Civil War and the abolishment of slavery, Georgia further developed its railroads, ports, and industry. The larger cities, such as Atlanta, Macon, Savannah, Augusta, and Columbus, became important factory, mill, and shipping centers. A new URBAN (city-based) culture, dependent on industry, took its place alongside the rural farming culture that had dominated in the past.

AS ATLANTA'S HISTORIC SITES AND BUILDINGS ARE DEMOLISHED TO MAKE ROOM FOR HIGHWAYS, DEPARTMENT STORES, AND A SUBWAY, ARCHAEOLOGISTS ARE ON THE JOB MAKING PHOTOGRAPHS AND SALVAGING ARTIFACTS SO THAT THEY CAN BE STUDIED LATER.

ARCHAEOLOGISTS IN GEORGIA HAVE MUCH TO LEARN FROM SITES THAT ARE NOT ASSOCIATED WITH PREHISTORIC CULTURES. THIS FIELD OF <u>HISTORICAL ARCHAEOLOGY</u> IS GROWING EVERY DAY. RECENT STUDIES HAVE BEEN MADE OF SLAVE SITES ON GEORGIA'S COASTAL ISLANDS. THE CABIN SITES OF RURAL WHITE FARMERS, AND CIVIL WAR BATTLE SITES HAVE BEEN EXPLORED IN NORTHERN GEORGIA. IN ATLANTA, THE REMAINS OF URBAN GARBAGE DUMPS FROM THE EARLY 1900'S ARE BEING SCIENTIFICALLY EXCAVATED JUST AHEAD OF THE CONSTRUCTION OF SHOPPING CENTERS AND NEW OFFICE BUILDINGS.

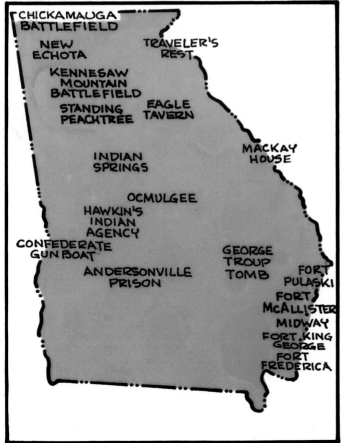

THESE RECENT SITES ARE IMPORTANT BECAUSE THEY CONTAIN INFORMATION THAT HAS NOT BEEN RECORDED IN WRITTEN DOCUMENTS. THE WRITTEN RECORDS WE HAVE ARE ESPECIALLY LACKING IN INFORMATION ABOUT THE DAILY LIVES OF AVERAGE PEOPLE. EVEN FOR THE EARLY 1900'S — JUST A FEW GENERATIONS AGO — THERE ARE LARGE GAPS IN OUR KNOWLEDGE ABOUT THE CULTURE OF WORKING CLASS AMERICANS. IN SUCH CASES, GARBAGE DUMPS BECOME MUCH LIKE DIARIES BURIED IN THE GROUND. THEREFORE, ARCHAEOLOGISTS ARE NEEDED WHEREVER THERE IS IMPORTANT INFORMATION TO BE UNEARTHED, REGARDLESS OF THE AGE OF THE SITES.

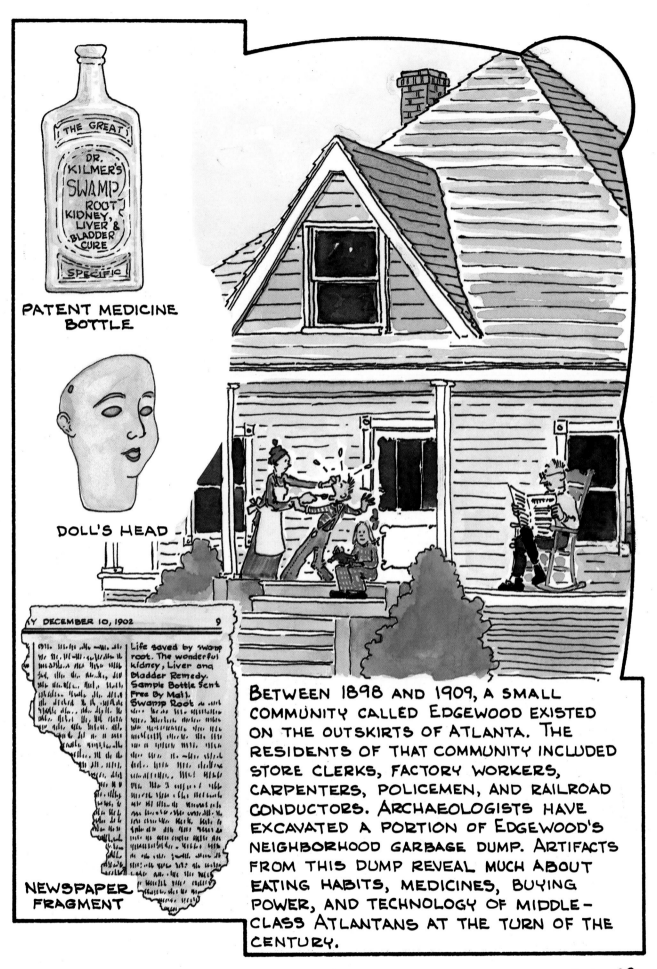

THE GREAT
DR. KILMER'S
SWAMP
ROOT
KIDNEY,
LIVER &
BLADDER
CURE
SPECIFIC

PATENT MEDICINE BOTTLE

DOLL'S HEAD

Y DECEMBER 10, 1902   9

Life saved by swamp root. The wonderful kidney, Liver and Bladder Remedy. Sample Bottle Sent Free By Mail. Swamp Root

NEWSPAPER FRAGMENT

BETWEEN 1898 AND 1909, A SMALL COMMUNITY CALLED EDGEWOOD EXISTED ON THE OUTSKIRTS OF ATLANTA. THE RESIDENTS OF THAT COMMUNITY INCLUDED STORE CLERKS, FACTORY WORKERS, CARPENTERS, POLICEMEN, AND RAILROAD CONDUCTORS. ARCHAEOLOGISTS HAVE EXCAVATED A PORTION OF EDGEWOOD'S NEIGHBORHOOD GARBAGE DUMP. ARTIFACTS FROM THIS DUMP REVEAL MUCH ABOUT EATING HABITS, MEDICINES, BUYING POWER, AND TECHNOLOGY OF MIDDLE-CLASS ATLANTANS AT THE TURN OF THE CENTURY.

CHAPTER III

AN ARCHAEOLOGICAL PROJECT

FIELD WORK

THE WORK OF AN ARCHAEOLOGIST BEGINS IN THE FIELD. OFTEN YOU READ ABOUT THIS PHASE OF HIS WORK IN NEWSPAPERS AND MAGAZINES, BUT FIELD WORK IS ONLY ONE PART OF A COMPLETE PROJECT. A LARGE CREW, WORKING SEVERAL MONTHS, CAN ACCUMULATE ENOUGH <u>DATA</u> (INFORMATION) TO KEEP AN ARCHAEOLOGIST AND A LARGE LABORATORY STAFF BUSY FOR TWO OR THREE YEARS. THE END RESULT OF ALL THIS LABOR IS A FINAL REPORT. THIS REPORT, WHICH CONTAINS ALL OF THE FINDINGS FROM A PROJECT, IS SENT TO MANY ARCHAEOLOGISTS AND OTHER SCIENTISTS SO THAT THEY MAY ADD TO THEIR OWN KNOWLEDGE.

IN THIS CHAPTER, WE WISH TO TAKE YOU ON AN ARCHAEO-
LOGICAL EXCAVATION, CALLED A "DIG" FOR SHORT. OUR DIG IS
SMALL, HAVING ONLY ONE ARCHAEOLOGIST AND A FEW STUDENTS,
BUT REMEMBER THAT DOZENS OF ARCHAEOLOGISTS AND HUNDREDS
OF STUDENTS HAVE WORKED MANY YEARS TO BUILD A BODY OF
KNOWLEDGE ABOUT GEORGIA'S PAST. WE WILL GATHER NEW DATA
FROM OUR EXCAVATION AND THEN WE WILL STUDY REPORTS
PUBLISHED BY OTHER ARCHAEOLOGISTS. FROM THESE TWO SOURCES,
WE CAN INTERPRET WHAT OUR SITE MIGHT HAVE BEEN LIKE
HUNDREDS OF YEARS AGO.

ANOTHER VERY IMPORTANT THING TO KEEP IN MIND IS THAT
THE WORK OF RECONSTRUCTING THE PAST IN GEORGIA HAS HARDLY
BEGUN. THERE ARE HUNDREDS OF KNOWN SITES THAT HAVE NOT
YET BEEN SCIENTIFICALLY STUDIED, AND THERE ARE PROBABLY
MANY HUNDREDS MORE STILL UNDISCOVERED. REMEMBER THAT YOU
CAN PLAY AN IMPORTANT PART IN BRINGING NEW SITES TO THE
ATTENTION OF ARCHAEOLOGISTS. WE WILL TELL YOU HOW TO DO
THIS LATER IN THE BOOK.

TODAY, WE ARE STANDING IN A FIELD WITH THE LAND OWNER AND AN ARCHAEOLOGIST. THE LAND OWNER HAS KINDLY GIVEN US PERMISSION TO USE PART OF HIS FIELD FOR OUR DIG. WHY HAVE WE CHOSEN THIS PARTICULAR FIELD?

SEVERAL MONTHS AGO, SHORTLY AFTER THE FIELD WAS PLOWED, THE ARCHAEOLOGIST FLEW OVER IT IN AN AIRPLANE AND MADE AERIAL PHOTOGRAPHS. IN THE ILLUSTRATION BELOW YOU CAN CLEARLY SEE A DARK AREA IN THE MIDDLE OF THE FIELD. THE ARCHAEOLOGIST DECIDED THAT THE DARK AREA MIGHT BE AN ARCHAEOLOGICAL SITE. PROBABLY THIS IS WHERE AN INDIAN VILLAGE ONCE STOOD. THE DARK STAIN IN THE SOIL WOULD BE CAUSED BY CHARCOAL FROM ANCIENT FIREPLACES, FOOD REMAINS, BROKEN TOOLS, AND OTHER ARTIFACTS. THIS STAIN COULD BE EASILY RECOGNIZED WHEN THE SITE WAS VIEWED FROM THE AIR, AND ESPECIALLY AFTER THE FIELD HAD BEEN FRESHLY PLOWED.

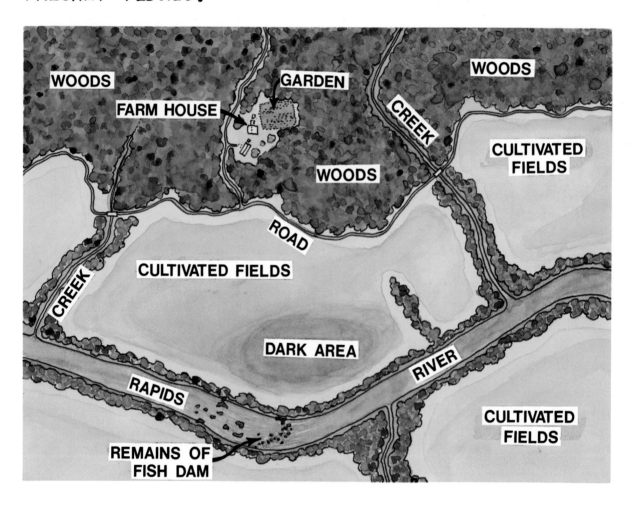

AERIAL VIEW OF THE ARCHAEOLOGICAL SITE AND SURROUNDING AREA AS IT APPEARS TODAY.

In prehistoric times, the river was not POLLUTED (spoiled by large amounts of waste) as it is today. Fresh water clams and other shellfish could have been collected from shallow waters around the rapids. Also, fish could have been caught easily by building a V-shaped stone dam across the river. Fish and shellfish were very important sources of meat to supplement the vegetable products grown on the floodplain. The hills, valleys and swamps located inland from the floodplain also contained animals that could be hunted and wild plants that could be collected by the Indians.

Now you can see why we would expect to find an Indian site in this field. The villagers could have obtained food from agriculture, hunting, fishing, and plant gathering, all near this one location.

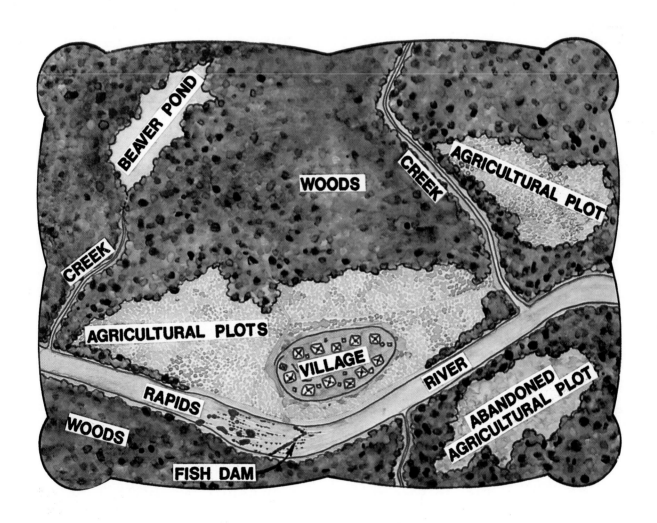

Reconstructed view of the same area in prehistoric times. Compare this view with the one on the opposite page.

After examining the aerial photographs, the archaeologist and his students obtained permission from the land owner to visit the field and make a surface collection. They found potsherds, broken stone tools, and fragments of animal bones. They had found an archaeological site! They gave the site a number, 9Fu300. "9" was for the state of Georgia. "Fu" was for Fulton County, and "300" because it was the 300th site recorded in Fulton County. The bags of artifacts from our surface collection were all labeled "9Fu300-surface."

Surface Collecting

We have already seen how pottery can be used for dating the past. Much of the pottery we found in this field looked like the example below. By comparing the characteristics of these potsherds with those from other sites, we know that this style was being made in Georgia about A.D. 1500.

Our site is on the river floodplain. Each time the river floods, a thin layer of ALLUVIUM (sand and clay) is left behind. This alluvium is naturally very fertile. Indians recognized this fact thousands of years ago. Gradually, as agricultural products came to provide more of their food supply, the Indians selected floodplains for their gardens and their villages. Our site is on the highest part of the floodplain, a spot that would not have been flooded as often as other areas around it.

THE ARCHAEOLOGIST CHOSE THIS SITE FOR OUR DIG BECAUSE THE ARTIFACTS IN THE SURFACE COLLECTION INDICATED THAT THE VILLAGE WAS OCCUPIED ABOUT A.D. 1500, IN THE MISSISSIPPIAN PERIOD. THIS WAS JUST BEFORE INDIANS CAME INTO CONTACT WITH EUROPEAN EXPLORERS AND COLONISTS. SITES OF THIS PERIOD NEED TO BE STUDIED SO WE CAN COMPARE THEM WITH SITES OCCUPIED DURING THE HISTORIC PERIOD. YOU HAVE SEEN HOW INDIAN CULTURE WAS CHANGED BY CONTACT WITH EUROPEANS.

IMAGINE THAT YOU ARE JOINING US ON THIS DIG. YOU WILL BE FAMILIAR WITH MOST OF THE TOOLS USED BY ARCHAEOLOGISTS. SOME COMMON TOOLS ARE SHOVELS, WHEELBARROWS, SMALL BRICKLAYERS' TROWELS, AND PAINT BRUSHES. SOME NOT SO COMMON TOOLS ARE SURVEYING INSTRUMENTS AND LARGE SIFTERS. THE WORK WILL BE HARD, BUT WE HOPE IT WILL BE REWARDING AND THAT WE WILL MAKE A CONTRIBUTION TO OUR KNOW-LEDGE ABOUT PREHISTORIC GEORGIANS.

ESTABLISHING THE GRID

THE FIRST STEP IN OUR DIG IS TO MEASURE THE AREA TO BE EXCAVATED INTO 3-METER (ABOUT 10-FOOT) SQUARES. OUR MEASURING IS DONE VERY CAREFULLY WITH SURVEYING INSTRUMENTS. WE THEN PLACE WOODEN STAKES AT THE CORNERS OF EACH SQUARE, AND STRING IS STRETCHED BETWEEN THE STAKES. WHEN WE HAVE FINISHED THIS MEASURING, AND HAVE PLACED OUR STAKES AND STRING, THE SITE WILL LOOK LIKE A GIANT CHECKERBOARD. THIS IS CALLED A "GRID."

EACH SQUARE OF OUR GRID IS GIVEN A SEPARATE NUMBER. WE WILL USE THESE NUMBERS THROUGHOUT THE DIG, AND WE WILL REFER TO THEM WHEN WE RETURN TO THE LABORATORY. REMEMBER THAT THE ARCHAEOLOGIST MUST BE ABLE TO IDENTIFY THE EXACT LOCATION OF EACH ARTIFACT AND GROUPS OF ARTIFACTS AFTER THEY HAVE BEEN REMOVED FROM THEIR ORIGINAL POSITIONS. THE SQUARE NUMBERS ARE A PERMANENT RECORD OF ARTIFACT CONTEXT AND ASSOCIATION.

JEFF AND TOM, TWO MEMBERS OF OUR CREW, HAVE THE HONOR OF OPENING THE FIRST SQUARE, AND OUR DIG HAS BEGUN! YOU WILL NOTICE HOW JEFF AND TOM HAVE LEFT A <u>BALK</u> (A SMALL COLUMN OF DIRT) AROUND EACH GRID STAKE SO THAT IT WILL STAY IN PLACE THROUGHOUT THE DIG. THE NUMBER FOR EACH SQUARE IS RECORDED ON THE STAKE AT THE SOUTHEAST CORNER OF THAT SQUARE.

BALK

SQ. 1

JEFF AND TOM START TO FIND POTSHERDS ALMOST AT ONCE. CLAY POTS WERE USED FOR PREPARING, STORING AND SERVING FOOD. THESE POTS WERE VERY FRAGILE AND WE SHALL PROBABLY FIND THOUSANDS OF POTSHERDS IN OUR DIG THIS SUMMER. THERE WILL BE MANY OTHER ARTIFACTS OF CLAY, STONE OR BONE, AND POSSIBLY EVEN SOME OF WOOD AND CLOTH. WE WILL SAVE EVERY ARTIFACT THAT WE FIND SO THAT THEY CAN BE STUDIED AT THE LAB.

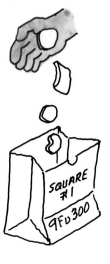

SQUARE #1
9FV 300

The first assignment for Jeff, Betty, and Tom is to remove the top layer of soil, which was disturbed by the farmer's plowing. At 9Fu300, this "PLOW ZONE" is 20 centimeters (about 8 inches) deep.

As Jeff and Tom dig, they shovel their dirt to Betty. Every shovel-full of dirt is sifted through a wire screen in order to recover all artifacts left by the villagers. For now, they will stop at the bottom of the plow zone. Below this level, they expect to find the undisturbed remains of this prehistoric village.

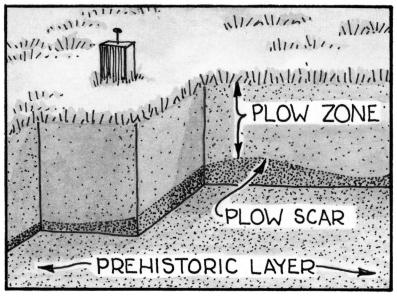

PLOW ZONE

PLOW SCAR

PREHISTORIC LAYER

Finally they have reached the bottom of the plow zone. In order to locate the village remains, they use a flat shovel, then a small brick-layer's trowel to scrape a smooth surface. You can see in the view above how this scraping has revealed changes in color and texture in the soil.

AFTER BETTY, TOM AND JEFF HAVE SCRAPED A CLEAN SURFACE IN THEIR SQUARE, THEY WILL PHOTOGRAPH AND MAP ALL SOIL CHANGES. THEY ALSO WILL PLACE EVERY ARTIFACT COLLECTED IN THIS SQUARE IN A BAG THAT IS LABELED BY SITE NUMBER, SQUARE, LEVEL, COLLECTOR, AND DATE. WE WILL REFER TO THE DRAWINGS, PHOTOS AND BAG LABELS WHEN WE RETURN TO THE LAB.

SQUARE #1

9Fu 300
SQ. 1
PLOW ZONE
BETTY, TOM,
JEFF
6·28-78

NOTEBOOK

A MAP IS MADE OF EACH SQUARE THAT IS EXCAVATED.

CAREFUL MEASURING IS VERY IMPORTANT IN MAKING THE MAPS.

EVERYTHING FOUND IN EACH SQUARE IS PUT INTO A MARKED BAG.

CAMERAS

PHOTOGRAPHS AND NOTES ARE AN IMPORTANT PART OF OUR WORK

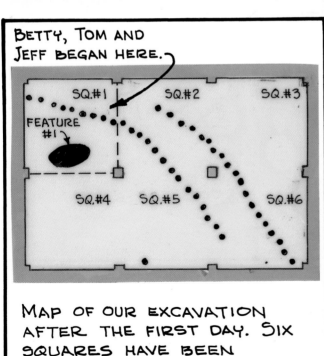

BETTY, TOM AND JEFF BEGAN HERE.

SQ.#1 SQ.#2 SQ.#3

FEATURE #1

SQ.#4 SQ.#5 SQ.#6

MAP OF OUR EXCAVATION AFTER THE FIRST DAY. SIX SQUARES HAVE BEEN UNCOVERED AND MAPPED.

WHILE JEFF AND TOM WERE DIGGING SQUARE NO. 1, BETTY WAS SIFTING THE EXCAVATED DIRT. OTHER MEMBERS OF THE CREW WERE OPENING SQUARES NOS. 2, 3, 4, 5 AND 6. AT THE END OF THE FIRST DAY, A MAP OF OUR DIG LOOKED LIKE THE PICTURE ON THE LEFT. TOM, BETTY AND JEFF HAD FOUND TWO VERY INTERESTING SOIL CHANGES BENEATH THE PLOW ZONE IN SQUARE NO. 1. THE FIRST IS A LARGE, OVAL DARK AREA. THIS IS THE FILLED IN REMAINS OF AN ANCIENT PIT. SUCH A PIT COULD BE A BURIAL CHAMBER, A TRASH PIT, A FOOD STORAGE PIT, OR A COOKING PIT. WE CALL THIS DARK AREA A "FEATURE" AND GIVE IT A NUMBER: FEATURE 1.

THE ARCHAEOLOGIST WORKS
WITH TOM AND JEFF TO CARE-
FULLY EXCAVATE FEATURE NO.1.
THEY BEGIN BY MARKING THE
EXACT OUTLINE OF THE DARK
AREA WITH THE POINT OF A
TROWEL. THEN THEY CAREFULLY
REMOVE THE DARK SOIL WHILE
WATCHING FOR ARTIFACTS THAT
MIGHT BE IN IT. AS THE WORK
PROGRESSES, THEY DISCOVER
THAT FEATURE NO.1 HAD BEEN A
SHALLOW PIT. ALL OF THE DIRT
FROM THIS FEATURE IS SIFTED
THROUGH FINE WIRE SCREEN IN
ORDER TO RECOVER SEEDS, BITS
OF ANIMAL BONE, AND OTHER
VERY SMALL ARTIFACTS. ONE
ARTIFACT JEFF FOUND IN THE
SCREEN WAS A SMALL FLINT
PROJECTILE POINT.

WHEN THEY REACH THE
BOTTOM OF FEATURE NO.1, THEY
FIND A NUMBER OF BROKEN
AND CRACKED PEBBLES. SOME
OF THE PEBBLES HAVE CHAR-
COAL ON THEM. THE ARCHAEO-
LOGIST, TOM AND JEFF AGREE
THAT FEATURE NO.1 PROBABLY
WAS A COOKING PIT THAT HAD
BEEN LINED WITH PEBBLES TO
RADIATE THE HEAT. AFTER THE
PIT WAS ABANDONED, THE
VILLAGERS HAD FILLED IT IN
WITH GARBAGE AND LOOSE
DIRT.

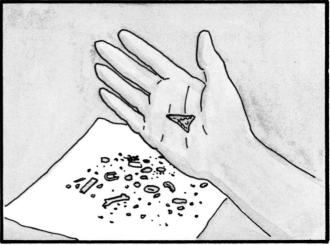

TO COMPLETE THEIR WORK,
JEFF, TOM AND THE ARCHAEOLO-
GIST MUST PHOTOGRAPH FEATURE
NO.1 AND MAKE ACCURATE
DRAWINGS OF IT. THESE PHOTOS
AND DRAWINGS WILL BE A
PERMANENT RECORD OF THEIR
WORK ON THIS ONE FEATURE.

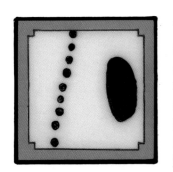

WE SAID TOM AND JEFF FOUND TWO INTERESTING THINGS IN SQUARE NO. 1. THE SECOND WAS A ROW OF SMALL, CIRCULAR, DARK STAINS. THESE STAINS ARE CALLED "POSTMOLDS." THEY ARE THE REMAINS OF WOODEN POSTS THAT WERE PLACED IN THE GROUND BY THE INDIANS. DUE TO THE MOIST CLIMATE IN GEORGIA, WOODEN POSTS DECAY RAPIDLY, LEAVING ONLY A STAIN IN THE SOIL. THE POSTMOLDS IN SQUARE NO. 1 MAY HAVE BEEN PART OF A HOUSE, A FENCE BETWEEN HOUSES, OR A STOCKADE THAT SURROUNDED THE VILLAGE. MORE SQUARES WILL HAVE TO BE EXCAVATED TO FIND THE COMPLETE PATTERN OF THESE POSTMOLDS.

DURING THE FIFTH WEEK OF OUR DIG, CARL AND CINDY BEGAN TO UNCOVER LARGE PIECES OF BURNED WOOD JUST BELOW THE PLOW ZONE IN SQUARE NO. 25. THE ARCHAEOLOGIST INSTRUCTED THE STUDENTS TO UNCOVER THESE REMAINS WITH GREAT CARE. THEY USED ONLY THEIR TROWELS, BRUSHES, AND OTHER SMALL TOOLS. THIS KIND OF WORK IS MUCH TOO DELICATE TO USE SHOVELS. ALL THE PIECES OF BURNED WOOD WERE EXPOSED IN THEIR EXACT POSITIONS. ALTOGETHER, THEY HAD TO CLEAR SIX SQUARES IN THIS MANNER. THEY HAD FOUND THE REMAINS OF A BURNED HOUSE. MIXED WITH THE CHARCOAL WERE TWO BROKEN POTS AND MANY OTHER ARTIFACTS. THIS INDICATED THAT THE HOUSE HAD NEVER BEEN REBUILT AFTER IT BURNED. WE LABELED THIS "HOUSE NO. 1." WE WILL SAY MORE ABOUT IT LATER.

BURNED HOUSE NO. 1 WITH CINDY, TOM AND CARL AT WORK.

DAY BY DAY, MORE SQUARES ARE OPENED. MOSTLY IT IS JUST HARD, STEADY WORK.

WE DIG,
SIFT,
PLACE ARTIFACTS IN MARKED BAGS,
SCRAPE,
MAP,
PHOTOGRAPH, AND
CAREFULLY EXCAVATE FEATURES AND POSTMOLDS.

OUR WORK MUST BE SYSTEMATIC SO THAT INFORMATION FROM ONE PART OF THE SITE CAN BE COMPARED WITH INFORMATION FROM ANY OTHER PART.

JEFF IS PHOTOGRAPHING FEATURE No. 1. RICK IS BRUSHING DIRT FROM FEATURE No. 2. CINDY IS USING TWO MEASURING TAPES TO LOCATE POSTMOLDS ON HER MAP. JIM IS SCRAPING THE FLOOR OF HIS SQUARE TO SEE IF HE CAN FIND MORE FEATURES.

AFTER MANY WEEKS OF STEADY PROGRESS WE HAVE UNCOVERED 70 SQUARES. OUR MAPS, PHOTOGRAPHS, BAGS AND NOTES HAVE BECOME AN EXCITING RECORD OF A PREHISTORIC VILLAGE. THIS RECORD HAS LAIN BENEATH THE SOIL OF GEORGIA FOR OVER 400 YEARS. WE HAVE FOUND **ARTIFACTS, FEATURES, BURIALS, AND POSTMOLDS.**

WE HAVE SAID THAT THE ARCHAEOLOGIST'S GOAL IS TO UNDERSTAND THE BEHAVIOR OF PEOPLE BY EXCAVATING AND STUDYING THEIR MATERIAL REMAINS. WE HAVE <u>EXCAVATED</u> A SET OF REMAINS. NOW, WE MUST GATHER UP OUR BAGS OF ARTIFACTS, OUR MAPS, AND OUR PHOTOS AND RETURN TO THE LAB TO BEGIN OUR <u>STUDY</u> OF THESE REMAINS.

THERE IS A FEELING OF SADNESS AS THE CREW LEAVES THE SITE ON THE LAST DAY OF THE DIG. WE DID NOT EXCAVATE THE ENTIRE SITE, BUT LEFT SOME AREAS UNDISTURBED FOR FUTURE ARCHAEOLOGISTS TO EXPLORE. WE BACKFILLED OUR EXCAVATIONS AND LEFT THE SITE JUST AS WE HAD FOUND IT.

LABORATORY WORK

The study and interpretation of the data from 9Fu300 will take place in the archaeology lab at Central City University, where the archaeologist teaches. Some of the students who worked on the dig will participate in the lab work. Others will graduate and be replaced by new students who are studying anthropology. Many important contributions will be made to archaeology by these students. Also, their education will be enriched by this experience in research.

The lab at Central City University

During the field work, we recorded all postmolds and features in each 3-meter square. Now that we are in the lab, we can sit down and put all of our maps together to see if we can find any patterns. After all of the squares have been included on one large map, we find that several patterns are present. We must remember that all of the postmolds on this master plan are nothing more than stains that tell us that a post once stood on that spot.

Four of the patterns show the remains of houses. Another appears to be the wall of a stockade that surrounded the village. There are many features, and there are quite a few postmolds that probably were from smaller structures, such as corn cribs, fences, or racks for drying meat or skins.

Now we will study each item found in the field. Through the rest of this chapter, we will refer many times to the Master Map of 9Fu300.

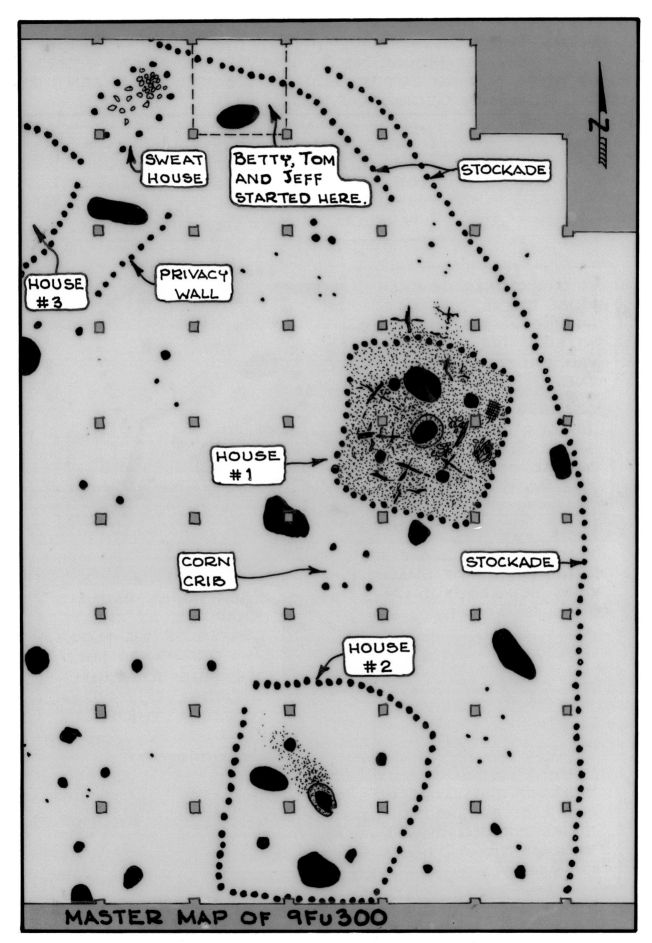

SWEAT HOUSE

BETTY, TOM AND JEFF STARTED HERE.

STOCKADE

HOUSE #3

PRIVACY WALL

HOUSE #1

CORN CRIB

STOCKADE

HOUSE #2

MASTER MAP OF 9Fu300

Look at the Master Map on Page 79. House No. 1 is the house that burned. We have the entire plan of House No. 2 and part of House No. 3. Let's take a walk through House No. 2 to find out something about a 15th century Indian house in Georgia.

THE BUILDERS OF THESE HOUSES DID NOT PLACE MUCH IMPORTANCE ON HAVING A PRECISELY SQUARE SHAPE. THE WALLS WERE SELDOM PARALLEL.

AT ONE CORNER OF EACH HOUSE THERE WAS AN OPENING IN THE POSTMOLD PATTERN. THE OPENING WAS PROBABLY A DOORWAY.

LARGER POSTS WERE USED INSIDE THE HOUSE TO HOLD UP THE ROOF.

THE OUTER WALLS WERE CONSTRUCTED OF SMALL POSTS SET ABOUT 15 CM (6 INCHES) APART.

EACH HOUSE HAD A FIREPLACE AT THE CENTER OF THE FLOOR. THE OCCUPANTS USED THE FIRE TO WARM THEMSELVES AND TO COOK THEIR FOOD.

SOME OF THE LARGE PITS ON THE FLOOR OF THE HOUSE TURNED OUT TO BE COOKING PITS AND FOOD STORAGE PITS. OTHERS WERE BURIAL CHAMBERS.

HOUSE #2

MAP OF HOUSE No. 2

HOUSE NO. 1 - A RARE FIND

AT THE TIME OUR VILLAGE WAS A THRIVING COMMUNITY, AN UNHAPPY EVENT OCCURRED. ONE OF THE HOUSES BURNED. AS FAR AS WE COULD TELL, THE OCCUPANTS ESCAPED, BUT MANY OF THEIR POSSESSIONS WERE LOST IN THE FIRE. SINCE THIS HOUSE HAD NOT BEEN REBUILT, ALL OBJECTS ON THE FLOOR WERE STILL IN THEIR ORIGINAL CONTEXT.

THE FIREPLACE WAS FILLED WITH ALL OF THE CHARCOAL FROM ITS LAST USE. THERE WERE TWO CRUSHED POTS NEAR THE FIREPLACE. A FLATTENED BASKET FILLED WITH CORN COBS WAS IN ONE CORNER. SOME REMNANTS OF WOVEN MATS, AND THE REMAINS OF FOOD THAT WAS BEING PREPARED JUST BEFORE THE HOUSE BURNED, WERE FOUND IN OTHER AREAS ON THE FLOOR.

IN THE LAB, THE REMAINS FROM THE FIREPLACE OF HOUSE NO. 1 ARE CAREFULLY WASHED. EVERYTHING IS PLACED IN A PAN WITH FINE SCREEN IN ITS BOTTOM. WATER IS SLOWLY POURED OVER IT SO THAT, IN A SHORT TIME, ALL THE DIRT HAS BEEN WASHED AWAY, LEAVING AN ASSORTMENT OF VERY SMALL ITEMS. A QUICK EXAMINATION OF SOME OF THESE ITEMS REVEALS TINY PIECES OF POTTERY AND BONE, CORN KERNELS, SEVERAL KINDS OF SEEDS, NUT SHELLS, AND PIECES OF INSECTS.

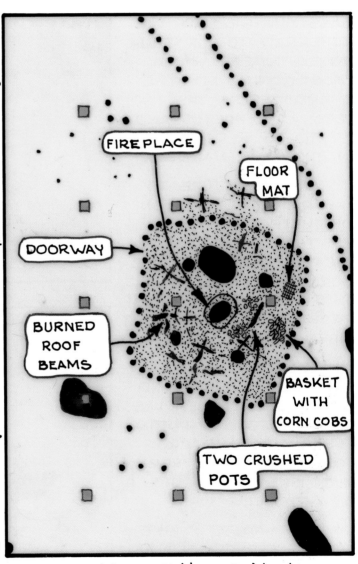

MAP OF HOUSE NO. 1

THE ENTIRE COLLECTION OF SMALL ITEMS IS CAREFULLY PACKED AWAY AND LATER WILL BE SENT TO SPECIALISTS FOR DETAILED STUDY. THE BONES WILL BE SENT TO A <u>ZOOLOGIST</u>, THE PLANT REMAINS TO A <u>BOTANIST</u>, AND THE INSECT REMAINS TO AN <u>ENTOMOLOGIST</u>. THE INFORMATION SUPPLIED BY THESE SPECIALISTS WILL BE INCLUDED IN THE FINAL REPORT ON 9Fu300.

THE TWO BROKEN POTS HAD BEEN EXCAVATED SO THAT ALL THE PIECES WERE RECOVERED. THE DIRT HAD BEEN CLEARED AWAY FROM THE SHERDS, EXPOSING THEM IN SITU (IN PLACE). DRAWINGS AND PHOTOGRAPHS HAD BEEN MADE, AND ALL THESE SHERDS PLACED IN SPECIALLY MARKED BAGS. IN THE LAB, WE REFERRED TO OUR FIELD NOTES TO SEE WHICH BAGS CONTAINED THE SHERDS FROM THE TWO POTS. OUR PHOTOS AND SKETCHES WERE FOUND IN THE SAME MANNER.

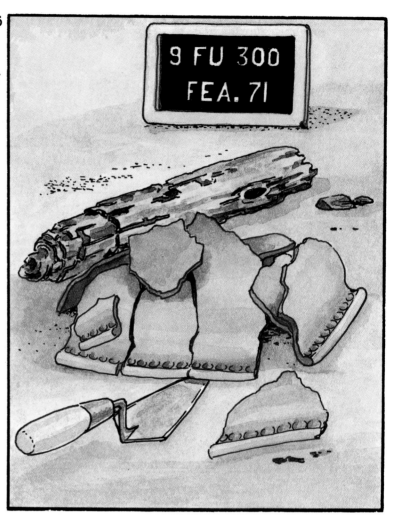

IN THE PICTURE TO THE RIGHT, WE SHOW ONE OF THE POTS IN ITS POSITION AS WE HAD EXCAVATED IT. NOTE THE BURNED ROOF BEAM IN THIS PICTURE. THIS BEAM PROBABLY BROKE THE POT WHEN THE ROOF FELL.

EACH SHERD WAS CAREFULLY WASHED AND LABELED. THEN JEFF WAS GIVEN THE JOB OF PUTTING THE TWO POTS BACK TOGETHER. IT WAS VERY MUCH LIKE DOING A JIGSAW PUZZLE.

JEFF HAD TO ATTEND HIS REGULAR CLASSES, DO HIS HOMEWORK, AND TAKE CARE OF ALL HIS OTHER RESPONSIBILITIES. THIS LEFT HIM ABOUT TWO HOURS EACH DAY FOR WORKING ON THE TWO POTS. THIS PROJECT TOOK HIM THREE WEEKS OF

CAREFUL WORK. AT LAST HE COULD PROUDLY SHOW OFF THE RESULTS OF HIS HARD WORK. HE HAD COMPLETELY RESTORED TWO POTS THAT HAD BEEN BROKEN OVER 400 YEARS AGO.

WHILE JEFF WAS RESTORING THE POTS, TOM AND ALICE HAD BEEN CONSTRUCTING AN EXHIBIT ABOUT OUR DIG AT 9Fu300. THIS EXHIBIT WILL BE PLACED IN THE LIBRARY AT THE UNIVERSITY SO THAT OTHER STUDENTS AND TEACHERS CAN LEARN ABOUT OUR WORK. THE TWO POTS THAT JEFF RESTORED, ALONG WITH OTHER ARTIFACTS, WILL BE PLACED IN THE EXHIBIT.

POTS RESTORED BY JEFF

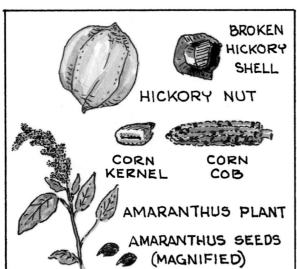

BROKEN HICKORY SHELL

HICKORY NUT

CORN KERNEL

CORN COB

AMARANTHUS PLANT

AMARANTHUS SEEDS (MAGNIFIED)

BECAUSE HOUSE NO. 1 HAD BURNED, THE REMAINS OF VEGETABLE FOODS THAT WERE BEING PREPARED FOR AN UPCOMING MEAL SURVIVED. VEGETABLE MATERIAL WILL STAY PRESERVED MUCH LONGER WHEN IT IS BURNED. AS WE SAID EARLIER, SOME OF THESE VEGETABLE REMAINS WERE SENT TO A BOTANIST AT A DISTANT UNIVERSITY FOR STUDY.

THE CHARRED REMAINS OF A BASKET WERE FOUND IN ONE CORNER OF HOUSE NO. 1. IT CONTAINED 14 CORN COBS. INDIANS MADE BASKETS IN GEORGIA FOR THOUSANDS OF YEARS. THEIR BASKETS CAME IN MANY SIZES AND SHAPES. THE ONE WE FOUND IN HOUSE NO. 1 WAS PROBABLY USED FOR COLLECTING AND STORING CORN FROM THE SURROUNDING GARDENS. THIS BASKET WAS MADE FROM STRIPS OF COMMON CANE. CANE LIKE THIS IS FOUND ALONG RIVERS AND STREAMS ALL OVER GEORGIA.

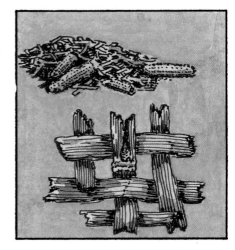

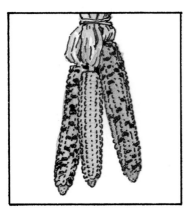

FINDING CORN IN HOUSE NO. 1 WAS NO SURPRISE. IT WAS MAINLY BECAUSE OF THIS REMARKABLE PLANT THAT A PERMANENT VILLAGE LIKE 9Fu300 WAS POSSIBLE. WE WOULD ALSO EXPECT TO FIND PUMPKIN, BEAN, AND SQUASH SEEDS, BECAUSE BY A.D. 1500 ALL THREE OF THESE PLANTS WERE GROWN IN GEORGIA. CERTAIN WILD PLANTS, SUCH AS AMARANTHUS (SOMETIMES CALLED "PIGWEED") WERE ALSO EATEN.

THE BURNED ROOF BEAMS HAD BEEN VERY CAREFULLY REMOVED TO THE LAB. WE CAN LEARN MUCH FROM THEM. FIRST, THEIR POSITIONS GIVE US VALUABLE CLUES AS TO HOW THE ROOF HAD BEEN BUILT. NEXT, WE CAN FIND OUT WHICH KIND OF WOOD HAD BEEN USED. AND, OF COURSE, SOME OF THIS CHARRED WOOD CAN BE USED FOR CARBON-14 DATING.

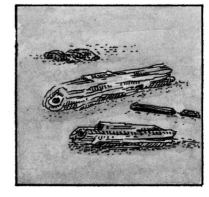

ON ONE AREA OF THE FLOOR OF HOUSE No. 1 WAS A FRAGMENT OF COPPER. A PIECE OF FINELY WOVEN CLOTH ABOUT 2 CENTIMETERS SQUARE WAS PRESERVED AGAINST THIS COPPER. A GEOLOGIST SAID THAT SALTS IN THE COPPER HAD HELPED TO PRESERVE THE FRAGILE CLOTH. WAS THE COPPER AND CLOTH PART OF CLOTHING?

INDIANS MADE USE OF COPPER FOR ORNAMENTS. THEY NEVER <u>SMELTED</u> METALS (MELTED THEM FROM ORE) BUT SIMPLY FOUND <u>NUGGETS</u> (SMALL PIECES OF PURE METAL) AND HAMMERED THESE NUGGETS INTO VARIOUS SHAPES. NUGGETS OF PURE COPPER CAN BE FOUND IN SEVERAL NORTH GEORGIA COUNTIES.

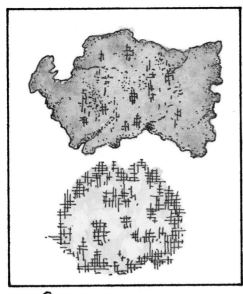

Copper and cloth

THE PIECE OF CLOTH THAT WAS PRESERVED AGAINST THE COPPER HAD A VERY FINE TEXTURE. THIS SHOWS THAT PREHISTORIC GEORGIA INDIANS HAD SOME TYPE OF LOOM FOR WEAVING. WHEN WE EXAMINED THE CLOTH UNDER A MICROSCOPE, WE FOUND THAT THE THREADS WERE MADE FROM THE FIBERS OF THE INNER BARK OF A BASSWOOD TREE. THERE ARE A NUMBER OF PLANTS IN GEORGIA THAT HAVE FIBERS SUITABLE FOR WEAVING.

PIECES OF WOVEN MAT WERE FOUND AT SEVERAL PLACES ON THE FLOOR OF HOUSE No. 1. THESE MATS WERE MADE FROM THE LEAVES OF CANE PLANTS. THESE LEAVES CAN BE FOLDED ONCE OR TWICE TO MAKE SOFT, PLIABLE STRIPS THAT CAN THEN BE WOVEN INTO MATS AND BASKETS.

WAS THE FLOOR OF THIS HOUSE COVERED WITH MATS IN THE SAME WAY THAT WE USE RUGS AND CARPETS?

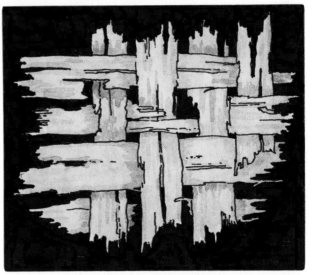

Cane leaf mat

WE FOUND SMALL PIECES OF ROPE MADE FROM GRAPE VINE, DEERSKIN AND INNER TREE BARK. SOME OF THE PIECES WERE STILL TWISTED AROUND THE CHARRED ROOF BEAMS SO THAT WE COULD SEE HOW THE ROOF MEMBERS WERE HELD TOGETHER. THE ROOF HAD BEEN <u>THATCHED</u> (COVERED IN LAYERS) WITH BROOM SEDGE. BROOM SEDGE IS A COMMON WEED THAT GROWS IN ALL PARTS OF GEORGIA.

AFTER WE HAD STUDIED THE REMAINS FROM HOUSE No. 1, ALONG WITH THE OTHER POSTMOLD PATTERNS, WE SET OUT TO MAKE A RECONSTRUCTION OF A TYPICAL HOUSE AT 9 Fu 300. TO ADD TO THE INFORMATION FROM OUR DIG, WE STUDIED THE DESCRIPTIONS OF INDIAN HOUSES IN THE WRITINGS OF EARLY EUROPEAN TRAVELERS AND EXPLORERS. THEN WE LOOKED AT REPORTS OF HOUSE REMAINS FOUND AT OTHER ARCHAEOLOGICAL SITES. THE RESULT OF OUR RECONSTRUCTION IS SHOWN ON THE OPPOSITE PAGE.

YOU CAN SEE THE LARGE HOLE IN THE CENTER OF THE ROOF. IT WAS THERE TO ALLOW SMOKE TO ESCAPE. WE HAD NO INFORMATION FROM OUR DIG FOR THIS HOLE, BUT THE HISTORIC ACCOUNTS SPEAK OF THEM FOR HOUSES OF SOUTHEASTERN INDIANS. THERE IS NO MENTION OF WINDOWS IN HISTORIC DESCRIPTIONS, SO THERE ARE NO WINDOWS IN OUR RECONSTRUCTION.

THIS RECONSTRUCTION WILL BE IN OUR FINAL REPORT. OTHER ARCHAEOLOGISTS WILL STUDY IT. WHEN THEY FIND A WELL PRESERVED HOUSE, THEY WILL TRY TO ADD TO, OR CHANGE, OUR INTERPRETATION.

THE ARCHAEOLOGIST STUDIES OLD DOCUMENTS TO LEARN ABOUT SOUTHEASTERN INDIAN CULTURE.

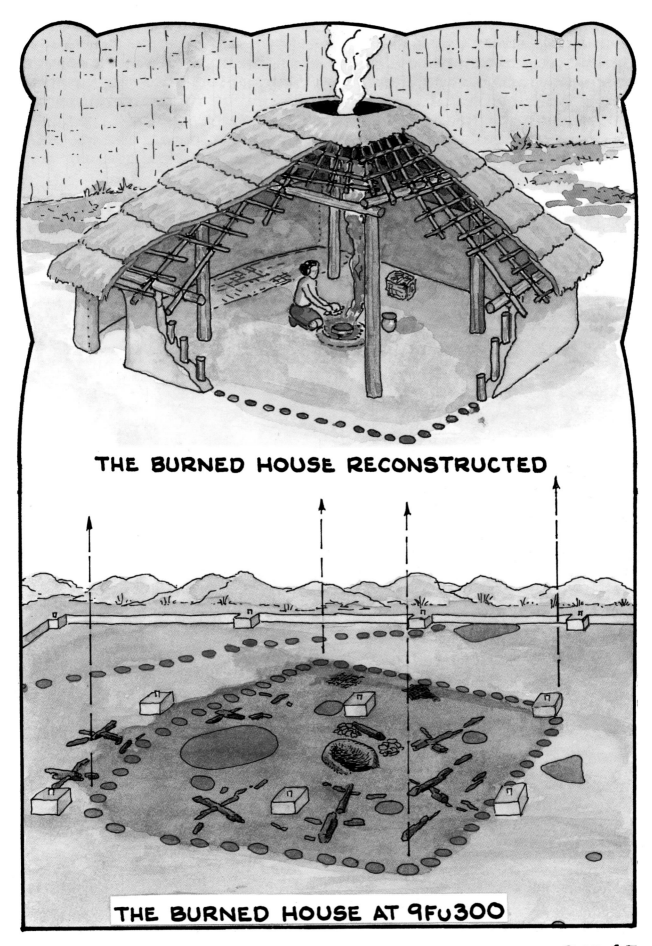

THE BURNED HOUSE RECONSTRUCTED

THE BURNED HOUSE AT 9Fu300

In Jeff's and Tom's first square, they found a row of postmolds that we at first thought was part of a house. But as we expanded our excavations, we found that the row continued across several squares. Finally, we decided that these postmolds had formed a stockade that surrounded the entire village. This stockade was made of logs 20 to 25 centimeters (about 8 to 10 inches) in diameter and spaced 20 centimeters (about 8 inches) apart.

Records of the 1539 to 1541 DeSoto expedition describe the wall around a large Indian town in southern Alabama. The records say: "*Situated upon a beautiful plain, the town of Mauvila was surrounded by a wall as high as three men and constructed of wooden beams. Plastered over was a mixture of thick mud tamped down with long straw.*"

Such walls were necessary for protection from surprise attacks of neighboring groups. Southeastern Indians practiced warfare on a limited basis.

PALISADE

Holes 2 or 3 feet deep were dug for each post. Vines were woven around the posts. Then, mud was plastered over the entire structure.

One interesting feature on our map was a row of post-molds located between House No. 1 and House No. 3 (see the Master Map on page 79). This row of postmolds probably formed a small wall between the houses during the time they were occupied.

By using cultural anthropology, we may be able to offer an explanation for this wall. Today, in certain parts of Africa, when neighboring families of a village have an argument, they may build a wall between them to signify that they are angry at one another. Although we do not know for sure if the wall at 9Fu300 was used for the same purpose as the "privacy wall" in Africa, it is one possible explanation.

Privacy Wall

CORN CRIB

LOOK AGAIN AT THE MASTER MAP ON PAGE 79. THERE IS A SMALL GROUP OF POSTMOLDS NEAR THE EAST WALL OF HOUSE No.1. THIS GROUP FORMS A RECTANGULAR PATTERN. THIS PATTERN MAY BE THE REMAINS OF A "CORN CRIB." WE KNOW FROM ACCOUNTS OF EARLY EXPLORERS THAT THE INDIANS OF THE SOUTHEAST HAD SUCH BUILDINGS FOR STORING THEIR VEGETABLE FOODS, ESPECIALLY CORN.

CORN CRIBS WERE RAISED WELL OFF THE GROUND ON STILTS. THEY WERE RAISED TO PROTECT THE CONTENTS FROM BEING EATEN BY DOGS OR RODENTS. STORED VEGETABLE FOODS WOULD COME IN HANDY DURING THE WINTER MONTHS WHEN OTHER FOODS WERE SCARCE.

ANOTHER COMMON BUILDING IN SOUTHEASTERN INDIAN VILLAGES WAS THE "SWEAT HOUSE." THE MASTER MAP ON PAGE 79 HAS THE REMAINS OF ONE OF THESE IN SQUARE NO. 2. WE HAVE A NUMBER OF ACCOUNTS FROM HISTORY OF THESE SWEAT HOUSES.

"Each house or habitation has besides a little conical house, covered with dirt, which is called the winter or hot house; this stands a few yards distant from the mansion-house, opposite the front door." THIS QUOTATION IS FROM THE DIARY OF WILLIAM BARTRAM, 1776. IN THIS PASSAGE, HE WAS DESCRIBING THE CHEROKEE TOWN OF COWEE IN WESTERN NORTH CAROLINA.

THESE SMALL EARTH-COVERED BUILDINGS WERE USED AS SWEAT BATHS. HOT ROCKS WERE BROUGHT INTO THE CENTER OF THE HOUSE AND WATER WAS POURED OVER THE ROCKS TO CREATE STEAM. THE INDIANS WOULD SIT AROUND THE WALLS OF THE HOUSE TO ALLOW THE STEAM TO MAKE THEM PERSPIRE. THIS SWEATING WAS THOUGHT TO CLEANSE A PERSON SPIRITUALLY AS WELL AS PHYSICALLY.

OUR PATTERN AT 9FU300 WAS A SMALL OVAL OF POSTMOLDS, WITH A CONCENTRATION OF ROCKS NEAR THE CENTER.

SWEAT HOUSE

REMEMBER THAT WE FOUND SEVERAL HUMAN BURIALS AT 9FU300. THESE WERE CAREFULLY EXCAVATED, AND THEIR CONTENTS WERE TAKEN TO THE LAB FOR PRESERVATION AND STUDY. THE ARCHAEOLOGIST'S INTEREST IN BURIALS IS NOT ONE OF MORBID CURIOSITY. BURIALS ARE A VERY IMPORTANT SOURCE OF KNOWLEDGE ABOUT PREHISTORIC PEOPLE.

WHEN BONES FROM A BURIAL ARE WELL PRESERVED, IT IS POSSIBLE TO TELL THE SEX AND APPROXIMATE AGE OF THE INDIVIDUAL. FOR INSTANCE THE SHAPE OF THE PELVIC (HIP) BONES TELL US WHETHER THE SKELETON IS A MALE OR FEMALE. WEAR PATTERNS ON THE TEETH AND THE DEGREE TO WHICH THE BONES ON THE SKULL CAP HAVE GROWN TOGETHER ARE CLUES TO THE AGE OF THE PERSON AT DEATH.

AN OLD PERSON'S TEETH WILL BE WORN DOWN MUCH MORE THAN A YOUNG ONE'S.

A HUMAN SKULL HAS 22 BONES. AT BIRTH, THESE BONES ARE SEPARATED, BUT AS A PERSON GROWS OLDER, THESE BONES GROW TOGETHER.

SOMETIMES AN AILMENT AND EVEN A CAUSE OF DEATH CAN BE DISCOVERED BY STUDYING THE BONES WE RECOVER. VITAMIN AND MINERAL DEFICIENCIES AFFECT THE TEETH AND BONES AND CAN

CLUES LIKE THESE HELP ARCHAEOLOGISTS TELL THE AGE OF A SKELETON.

BE DETECTED THROUGH CHEMICAL TESTS. ARTHRITIS, OSTEOMYLITIS, AND OTHER BONE DISEASES CAN BE DETECTED BY CLOSE STUDY OF BONE SURFACES.

EACH SKELETON AT 9FU300 WAS FOUND IN THE BURIAL PIT IN A FLEXED POSITION (LEGS AND ARMS BENT). DID THIS POSITION HAVE A RELIGIOUS AND SOCIAL MEANING, OR WAS IT JUST A WAY OF DISPOSING OF A HEAVY BODY WITH AS LITTLE WORK AS WAS POSSIBLE? MOST OF THE BURIALS WERE FOUND IN THE FLOORS OF THE HOUSES.

WHEN SEVERAL HUNDRED BURIALS OF A RELATED GROUP ARE FOUND AND STUDIED, WE CAN LEARN ABOUT THE PHYSICAL CHARACTERISTICS OF THE ENTIRE SOCIETY. FOR EXAMPLE, OVER 300 BURIALS HAVE BEEN RECOVERED FROM THE ETOWAH SITE NEAR CARTERSVILLE IN BARTOW COUNTY. IN ETOWAH SOCIETY, PEOPLE BELONGED EITHER TO A NOBLE CLASS OR A COMMON CLASS. PEOPLE OF THE COMMON CLASS WERE BURIED WITHIN THE TOWN, VERY MUCH LIKE WE FOUND AT 9FU300. BUT PEOPLE OF THE NOBLE CLASS WERE BURIED IN AND AROUND A SPECIAL TEMPLE MOUND. A STUDY OF THE REMAINS OF THESE TWO GROUPS SHOWS CLEARLY THAT THE NOBLE GROUP LIVED BETTER AND LONGER THAN THE COMMON PEOPLE.

ARTIFACTS FOUND IN A BURIAL, IN DIRECT ASSOCIATION WITH THE SKELETON, CAN PROVIDE VALUABLE DATA. THE BURIAL SHOWN BELOW HAD A NECKLACE OF SHELL BEADS. THE SHELL FOR THESE BEADS COMES FROM THE OCEAN. THEY MUST HAVE BEEN ACQUIRED FROM INDIANS LIVING ON THE GEORGIA, FLORIDA, OR ALABAMA COASTS.

THESE SHELL BEADS TELL US SOMETHING ABOUT THE TRADING HABITS OF THIS SOCIETY. WE CAN GO EVEN FURTHER AND STATE THAT IF OUR VILLAGERS TRADED WITH COASTAL PEOPLE, THEY PROBABLY EXCHANGED IDEAS AS WELL. SOMETIMES VERY IMPORTANT IDEAS, SUCH AS RECENT INVENTIONS, RELIGIOUS CONCEPTS, AND SOCIAL VALUES WERE EXCHANGED DURING TRADING EXPEDITIONS.

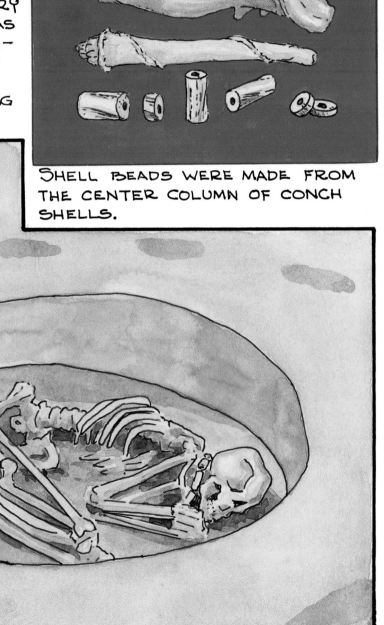

SHELL BEADS WERE MADE FROM THE CENTER COLUMN OF CONCH SHELLS.

9Fu300 BURIAL 4

ONCE WE HAVE COMPLETED THE LABORATORY ANALYSES OF THE ARTIFACTS, FEATURES, HOUSES, OTHER STRUCTURES, BURIALS, AND FOOD REMAINS, WE ARE READY TO RECONSTRUCT THE CULTURE OF 9Fu 300. WE SOON FIND THAT THE SEPARATE PIECES OF INFORMATION THAT WE HAVE RECOVERED FIT TOGETHER INTO A COMPLEX PICTURE OF A PAST CULTURE.

THE PEOPLE MADE USE OF MANY RAW MATERIALS FROM THEIR SURROUNDING ENVIRONMENT. THE FOREST ANIMALS PROVIDED FOOD FOR THE VILLAGERS. THE FOREST PLANTS WERE MADE INTO ROPES, BASKETS, HOUSES, AND CLOTHING. LOCAL CLAY WAS MADE INTO POTTERY. CERTAIN KINDS OF STONE WERE SHAPED INTO TOOLS. RICH GARDENS OF CORN, BEANS, SQUASH, AND PUMPKINS MADE IT POSSIBLE FOR SUCH A LARGE AND PERMANENT VILLAGE TO EXIST. THE STOCKADE SPEAKS CLEARLY OF DANGER, AND TELLS US THAT WARFARE WAS PART OF THE LIFE OF THESE PEOPLE. COOPERATION WAS ALSO PART OF THEIR CULTURE. OTHERWISE, THEY COULD NOT HAVE UNDERTAKEN THE BUILDING OF A STOCKADE, A FISH DAM, OR THE CLEARING AND CULTIVATION OF LARGE GARDENS.

THIS RECONSTRUCTION OF THE NOW-EXTINCT CULTURE AT 9Fu 300 WAS POSSIBLE ONLY BECAUSE THE ARCHAEOLOGIST RECOVERED AND STUDIED EVERY BIT OF INFORMATION. EVEN THE SMALLEST ARTIFACTS WERE NOT OVERLOOKED. THE RECONSTRUCTION ALSO WOULD NOT HAVE BEEN POSSIBLE IF THE RELATIONSHIPS (ASSOCIATION AND CONTEXT) OF THE REMAINS HAD NOT BEEN CAREFULLY OBSERVED AND RECORDED IN THE FIELD. IT WAS EVEN NECESSARY TO CALL UPON SPECIALISTS IN OTHER BRANCHES OF SCIENCE.

WHEN WE HAVE STUDIED ALL OF THE ARTIFACTS, FEATURES POST-MOLD PATTERNS, AND BURIALS FROM 9Fu300, WE WILL BE READY TO WRITE A FINAL REPORT. THIS REPORT WILL MAKE OUR FINDINGS AVAILABLE TO OTHER ARCHAEOLOGISTS AND TO ANYONE WHO IS INTERESTED IN PREHISTORIC GEORGIANS. THE SITE WE EXCAVATED IN THIS CHAPTER IS, OF COURSE, FICTIONAL. IT DOES REPRESENT A COMPOSITE OF DATA OBTAINED BY REAL ARCHAEOLOGISTS FROM REAL SITES. SUCH VILLAGE SITES HAVE BEEN EXCAVATED IN FULTON, BARTOW, CHEROKEE, FLOYD AND OTHER GEORGIA COUNTIES.

9Fu300 AS IT MIGHT HAVE APPEARED IN A.D. 1500 ➡

SITE 9FU300

FULTON COUNTY, GEORGIA

By Professor
R. A. Digwell

Assisted By
Tom Beasley
Jeff Mead
Betty Collins
Alice Tate

CENTRAL CITY UNIVERSITY
1978

When many village sites have been carefully excavated and the findings published, archaeologists can begin to reconstruct the complex story of Georgia's late prehistoric Indians. Then, the information from Georgia can be compared with information from other parts of the Southeast. Little by little the information grows. Bit by bit the giant "jigsaw puzzle" of the past is pieced together.

A project such as the one we have just described is not undertaken lightly. It takes trained people, time, money, and special facilities and equipment. Also, since new techniques are always being developed, the artifacts and field records from a project must be preserved so that they will be available to archaeologists of the future. Archaeology is an exciting and rewarding endeavor, but it is also one that places great responsibilities on those who practice it.

CHAPTER IV

YOU AND ARCHAEOLOGY

HOME AND CLASSROOM PROJECTS

MANY FASCINATING PROJECTS CAN BE BUILT AROUND AN INTEREST IN ARCHAEOLOGY. HERE ARE SEVERAL PROJECTS YOU CAN DO AT HOME OR IN THE CLASSROOM TO INCREASE YOUR KNOWLEDGE. SOME OF THESE PROJECTS MAY EVEN PROVIDE IMPORTANT INFORMATION TO PROFESSIONAL ARCHAEOLOGISTS WORKING IN YOUR AREA.

PROJECT NO. 1 MUCH OF THE PREHISTORIC REMAINS THAT ARCHAEOLOGISTS STUDY IS NOTHING MORE THAN TRASH AND GARBAGE. AT THE END OF THE DAY (OR WEEK), MAKE AN ARCHAEOLOGICAL STUDY OF THE MATERIAL REMAINS IN THE TRASH CAN IN YOUR ROOM AT HOME, OR IN YOUR CLASS-ROOM AT SCHOOL. BE SCIEN-TIFIC. BEGIN WITH THE ITEMS ON THE VERY TOP AND LIST EACH ONE AS IT IS REMOVED. IS THE TRASH STRATIFIED? IS THE OLDEST TRASH (IN THE

BOTTOM OF THE CAN) DIFFERENT FROM THE MIDDLE? OR TOP? IF THE REMAINS ARE DIFFERENT IN EACH LAYER, DOES THIS TELL YOU SOMETHING ABOUT YOUR ACTIVITIES DURING THAT DAY (OR WEEK)? WHAT KINDS OF HUMAN BEHAVIOR PRODUCED THIS TRASH? IF YOU COMPARED THE TRASH FROM YOUR ROOM WITH THE GARBAGE FROM YOUR KITCHEN, WOULD THERE BE MUCH DIFFERENCE?

PROJECT NO. 2 IN AMERICAN COMMUNITIES, PEOPLE EARN THEIR LIVING IN MANY DIFFERENT WAYS. THERE ARE FARMERS, STORE CLERKS, FACTORY WORKERS, CONSTRUCTION WORKERS, AND FISHERMEN. THERE ARE DOCTORS, LAWYERS, OFFICE WORKERS, AND DRAFTSMEN. EACH OCCU-PATION AFFECTS THE ENVIRONMENT IN A DIFFERENT WAY. FARMERS CLEAR FIELDS, PLOW THE EARTH, SPREAD FERTILIZER AND SEEDS, AND USE

MACHINES TO HARVEST THEIR CROPS. CHOOSE SEVERAL OCCUPATIONS AND MAKE A STUDY OF HOW EACH ONE AFFECTS THE ENVIRONMENT. DESCRIBE THE MATERIAL REMAINS (ARTIFACTS) EACH OCCUPATION LEAVES BEHIND. COULD ARCHAEOLOGISTS OF THE FUTURE RECONSTRUCT OUR CULTURE FROM THESE REMAINS?

PROJECT NO. 3 PREHISTORIC GEORGIANS USED MANY WILD PLANTS FOR FOOD, MEDICINE, DYES, WEAVING, AND CONSTRUCTION. MAKE A LIST OF THE USEFUL WILD PLANTS IN YOUR AREA. OLDER PEOPLE MAY REMEMBER HOW SOME OF THESE PLANTS WERE USED IN YEARS PAST. TELL WHAT PARTS OF EACH PLANT WERE IMPORTANT. HOW WERE THEY USED? COLLECT EXAMPLES AND MAKE A DISPLAY OF THEM. WATCH OUT FOR POISON IVY AND OTHER IRRITANT PLANTS!

PROJECT NO. 4 ON PAGE 108, ARE LISTED SOME OF THE GEORGIA PARKS THAT PRESERVE ARCHAEOLOGICAL SITES. IF YOU LIVE NEAR ONE OF THEM, VISIT IT AND MAKE A STUDY OF THAT SITE. DRAW A SKETCH MAP OF THE SITE. IF THERE ARE MOUNDS, BUILDINGS, OR OTHER FEATURES, SKETCH AND PHOTOGRAPH THEM. ASK FOR FREE PAMPHLETS, BROCHURES, OR OTHER INFORMATION ABOUT THE SITE. ASK THE PARK RANGER, HISTORIAN, OR SUPERINTENDENT TO TELL YOU ABOUT THE SITE AND WHY IT IS IMPORTANT TO THE HISTORY OR PREHISTORY OF GEORGIA. YOU CAN MAKE AN INTERESTING DISPLAY FROM THE PAMPHLETS, BROCHURES, DRAWINGS, AND PHOTOGRAPHS.

PROJECT NO. 5 FIND THE PEOPLE IN YOUR AREA WHO HAVE ARTIFACT COLLECTIONS. THERE ARE THOSE WHO COLLECT INDIAN ARTIFACTS, OLD FARM TOOLS, CIVIL WAR ITEMS, AND MANY OTHER MATERIAL REMAINS FROM THE PAST. THESE COLLECTIONS ARE OF LITTLE VALUE TO ARCHAEOLOGY UNLESS WE KNOW WHERE THEY WERE FOUND, WHEN THEY WERE FOUND, AND WHO FOUND THEM. VISIT THE COLLECTORS AND MAKE LISTS OF THEIR ARTIFACTS. ASK THEM WHERE, WHEN, AND BY WHOM THE ARTIFACTS WERE FOUND. MAKE SKETCHES AND DRAWINGS. SEND YOUR LISTS, DRAWINGS AND COMMENTS TO THE NEAREST ARCHAEOLOGIST.

HOW TO REPORT A SITE

If you should find an archaeological site, the most important thing to remember is: <u>Do not dig in or disturb the site.</u> Report it to an archaeologist and then help protect it. Most of the time, the archaeologist will not want to rush in and excavate your site. Instead, he or she will want to record its location, so that sometime in the future it can be carefully studied. If your site is being destroyed, be sure to state this clearly in your report and explain how the destruction is taking place. Do not remove artifacts from the site—even from the surface. An archaeologist can learn a great deal more from the site by seeing it with the artifacts in place.

Page 102 shows a site report that has been filled out with the information needed by an archaeologist. We have used a ficticious site as an example. You can make your own forms on notebook paper. After you have filled out the form for your site, send it to the nearest archaeologist. There is a list of archaeological departments and museums on page 103. You should keep in mind that most archaeologists are involved in many projects. It may be some time before

YOU RECEIVE A REPLY, BUT REST ASSURED THAT YOUR REPORT WILL BE APPRECIATED! IF THE SITE IS IMPORTANT ENOUGH, THE ARCHAEOLOGIST OR ONE OF HIS ASSISTANTS MAY COME TO SEE IT.

YOUR REPORT SAYS, "I AM A RESPONSIBLE CITIZEN, AND I WANT TO TAKE PART IN THE PRESERVATION AND STUDY OF MY HERITAGE."

HOW TO SKETCH AN ARTIFACT

THERE ARE MANY KINDS OF ARTIFACTS. SOMETIMES THE BEST WAY TO DESCRIBE THEM IS BY MAKING A DRAWING.

IF YOU HAVE A POTSHERD, FOR EXAMPLE, AND YOU WANT TO SKETCH IT, LAY IT ON A PIECE OF PAPER AND TRACE AROUND IT. THEN, IF THERE IS A DESIGN ON IT, DRAW THE DESIGN AS ACCURATELY AS YOU CAN.

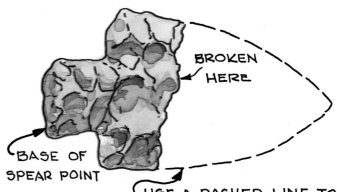

BROKEN HERE

BASE OF SPEAR POINT

USE A DASHED LINE TO SHOW HOW YOU THINK THE REMAINDER LOOKED.

IF YOU HAVE AN ARTIFACT THAT IS BROKEN, LOOK AT PICTURES OF WHOLE ONES TO SEE WHAT THE ENTIRE PIECE LOOKED LIKE. THEN USE DASHED LINES TO FILL IN THE MISSING PART. SOME BROKEN ARTIFACTS WILL BE QUITE A PUZZLE, BUT IF YOU PERSIST, YOUR KNOWLEDGE AND UNDER-STANDING WILL GROW. BE SURE TO INCLUDE YOUR SKETCHES WITH YOUR REPORT FORM.

SITE REPORT FORM

YOUR NAME _R. A. DIGWELL_

YOUR ADDRESS _2278 JOHNSON RD. ——————, GA. 30099_

PHONE NUMBER _998-4948_

DATE _JANUARY 1, 1978_

TELL HOW TO GET TO THE SITE. _4 MILES NORTH OF JONES, GA., ON_ _HIGHWAY 170. TURN WEST ON YEHAW RD. AT UNITY CHURCH AND GO_ _TO RIVER. SITE IS ON HIGHEST GROUND IN THE FLOODPLAIN. THE_ _SIZE OF SITE IS ABOUT 3 ACRES._

NAME OF OWNER OF SITE _RICHARD A. PALMER_

OWNER'S ADDRESS _ROUTE 1, JONES, GA._

DRAW A MAP SHOWING HOW TO GET TO THE SITE. BE SURE TO INCLUDE NEARBY RIVERS OR CREEKS, ROADS, CHURCHES, SCHOOLS, AND OTHER LANDMARKS THAT WILL HELP THE ARCHAEOLOGIST FIND THE SITE.

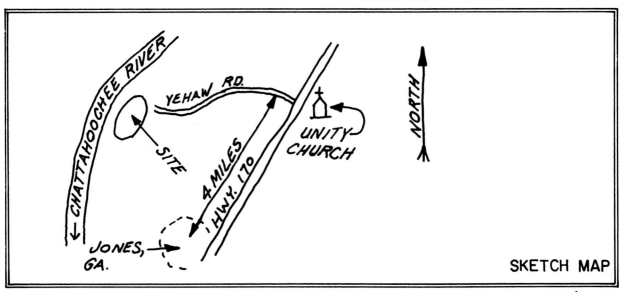

SKETCH MAP

DESCRIBE THE ARTIFACTS YOU OBSERVED ON THE SITE, BUT DON'T REMOVE THEM FROM THE SITE. ATTACH PHOTOGRAPHS OF THE SITE IF YOU HAVE ANY. _POTSHERDS AND A BROKEN PROJECTILE POINT WERE_ _OBSERVED ON THE SURFACE OF THE SITE. SKETCHES_ _OF THE ARTIFACTS ARE ATTACHED TO THIS REPORT._

Many important sites have been discovered and first reported by people who were not professional archaeologists. For this reason, we have listed some of the universities and museums where you can report sites and collections

Universities and Museums with Archaeologists.

Columbus Museum
Columbus, Georgia 31906
(706) 649-0713

Department of Anthropology
and Geography
Georgia State University
Atlanta, Georgia 30303
(404) 651-3232

Department of History and
Anthropology
Augusta State University
Augusta, Georgia 30904
(706) 737-1709

Laboratory of Archaeology
Department of Anthropology
State University of West Georgia
Carrollton, Georgia 30118
(770) 836-6455

Division of Arts and Sciences
Thomas University
Thomasville, Georgia 31792
(229) 226-1621

Department of Sociology and
Anthropology
Georgia Southern University
Statesboro, Georgia 30460
(912) 681-5443

Laboratory of Archaeology
Department of Anthropology
University of Georgia
Athens, Georgia 30602
(706) 542-3922

Department of Sociology and
Anthropology
Valdosta State University
Valdosta, Georgia 31698
(229) 333-5943

Sources for More Information on Archaeology in Georgia

Office of the State Archaeologist
Historic Preservation Division
Atlanta, Georgia 30303
(404) 656-9344

Society for Georgia Archaeology
P.O. Box 693
Athens, Georgia 30603
(678) 287-5814

A STRATIGRAPHIC BOX

YOU OR YOUR CLASS CAN CONDUCT AN EXPERIMENT THAT WILL SHOW YOU HOW ARCHAEOLOGISTS STUDY STRATIGRAPHY ON REAL ARCHAEOLOGICAL SITES. YOU WILL NEED THE FOLLOWING EQUIPMENT:

1. AQUARIUM OR PLASTIC PLANTER — ABOUT 10 GALLON SIZE.
2. A BAGFUL OF CLEAN SAND.
3. NOTEBOOK PAPER, GLUE OR TAPE, SPOON, TABLE KNIFE, METRIC RULER, TEA STRAINER, 5 SMALL PAPER BAGS, SCISSORS, PENCIL OR PEN, A SMALL FUNNEL, A MEASURING CUP, AND A MIXING PAN.
4. FIVE ONE-POUND CANS OF DRY TEMPERA PAINT. BLACK, BROWN, RED, YELLOW, AND BLUE.
5. FIVE TUBES OF SMALL, COLORED BEADS. GREEN, ORANGE, PURPLE, PINK, AND LIGHT BLUE.

MAKING A STRATIGRAPHIC SEQUENCE

STEP 1. POUR A LAYER OF PLAIN SAND IN THE BOTTOM OF THE BOX TO A DEPTH OF 3 CM. SMOOTH THE LAYER WITH THE KNIFE.

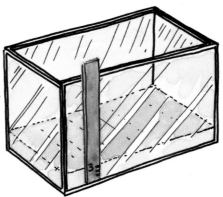

COUNT THE NUMBER OF CUPS OF SAND THAT IT TOOK TO MAKE THIS 3 CM LAYER.

STEP 2. MEASURE ENOUGH PLAIN SAND INTO THE MIXING PAN TO MAKE ANOTHER 3 CM LAYER. COLOR THIS SAND RED WITH TEMPERA PAINT. POUR IN THE TUBE OF LIGHT BLUE BEADS AND STIR UNTIL WELL MIXED. NOW CAREFULLY SPREAD THIS RED SAND ON TOP OF THE PLAIN SAND AND SMOOTH. IF YOU MEASURED THE CORRECT NUMBER OF CUPS OF SAND, THIS LAYER WILL BE 3 CM THICK.

STEP 3. CUT 12 STRIPS OF NOTEBOOK PAPER TO 5 CM BY 14CM EACH. ROLL EACH STRIP TO MAKE TUBES THAT MEASURE 1.5 CM IN DIAMETER.

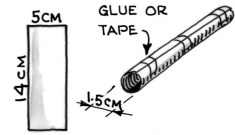

5CM

14CM

GLUE OR TAPE

1.5CM

STEP 4. NOW ARRANGE THE TUBES IN A CRUDE CIRCLE IN THE BOX AND PUSH THEM INTO THE SAND SO THAT 8CM OF EACH TUBE IS LEFT STANDING ABOVE THE RED SAND. NEXT, MIX A MEASURING CUPFUL OF SAND WITH BLACK TEMPERA. USE A LOT OF BLACK IN THIS MIXTURE. TAKE THE FUNNEL AND POUR 6CM OF BLACK SAND INTO EACH TUBE.

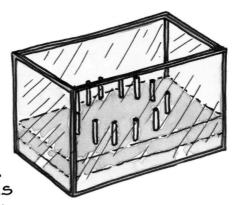

STEP 5. MIX ANOTHER 3 CM THICK LAYER OF SAND. THIS TIME, USE BROWN TEMPERA COLOR AND PINK BEADS. WHEN YOU SPREAD THIS LAYER, BE CAREFUL NOT TO GET ANY BROWN SAND INTO THE TUBES.

STEP 6. MIX ANOTHER 3 CM LAYER USING YELLOW TEMPERA COLOR AND PURPLE BEADS. SPREAD AND SMOOTH. THIS WILL BE TO THE TOP OF THE BLACK SAND INSIDE THE TUBES. NOW, SLOWLY REMOVE THE PAPER TUBES. TAP ON THE TUBES LIGHTLY WITH YOUR FINGER AS YOU PULL THEM OUT SO THAT ALL OF THE BLACK SAND STAYS IN THE HOLES CREATED BY THE TUBES.

STEP 7. MIX A SMALL AMOUNT OF BLACK TEMPERA COLOR INTO ANOTHER 3CM LAYER OF SAND. ADD ORANGE BEADS. SPREAD AND SMOOTH. MIX A 3CM LAYER COLORED WITH BLUE AND ADD GREEN BEADS. SPREAD AND SMOOTH.

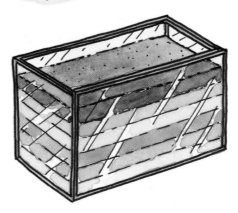

YOU HAVE COMPLETED THE STRATIGRAPHIC SEQUENCE. NOW, YOU ARE READY TO EXCAVATE.

EXCAVATING THE STRATIGRAPHIC BOX

STEP 1. LABEL A SHEET OF NOTEBOOK PAPER, <u>STRATIGRAPHIC PROFILE</u>. THEN, MAKE A A DRAWING OF ONE END OF THE BOX SHOWING ALL THE LAYERS. MEASURE THEIR THICKNESSES WITH YOUR RULER AND NOTE THIS ON THE DRAWING. NOTE THE COLOR OF EACH LAYER ON YOUR DRAWING. THE TOP LAYER IS MARKED "LAYER 1." THE SECOND LAYER IS MARKED "LAYER 2." THE NEXT IS "LAYER 3", ON DOWN TO THE BOTTOM, WHICH IS "LAYER 6." NOW LABEL ANOTHER SHEET OF NOTEBOOK PAPER, <u>FIELD NOTES</u>. YOU WILL RECORD EVERYTHING YOU DO ON THIS SHEET.

STEP 2. USING THE SPOON, EXCAVATE LAYER 1. BE VERY CAREFUL TO DIG ONLY THE BLACK LAYER OF SAND. SIFT ALL THE SAND FROM LAYER 1 THROUGH THE TEA STRAINER TO RECOVER THE BEADS. PLACE THESE BEADS IN A PAPER BAG MARKED "LAYER 1". WHEN YOU THINK YOU HAVE REACHED THE BOTTOM OF THE FIRST LAYER, STOP DIGGING AND SEAL THE BAG. IN YOUR FIELD NOTES, DESCRIBE WHAT YOU HAVE JUST DONE.

STEP 3. EXCAVATE LAYER 2 IN EXACTLY THE SAME MANNER. SIFT THE SAND AND PLACE THE BEADS IN A PAPER BAG MARKED "LAYER 2." NOTE THE COLOR OF BEADS IN THE STRATIGRAPHIC PROFILE. WHEN YOU REACH THE BOTTOM OF LAYER 2, TAKE THE TABLE KNIFE AND LIGHTLY SCRAPE THE TOP OF LAYER 3. YOU WILL SEE THE 12 CIRCLES OF BLACK SAND APPEAR. ENTER ALL OF THIS IN YOUR FIELD NOTES.

STEP 4. TAPE 2 SHEETS OF NOTEBOOK PAPER TOGETHER AND LABEL IT <u>POSTMOLD PATTERN</u>. 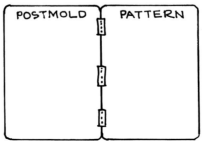 THIS SHEET WILL BE THE MAP OF YOUR SITE. NOW CAREFULLY MEASURE THE POSTMOLD PATTERN IN THE STRATIGRAPHIC BOX AND, THEN, USING

THESE MEASUREMENTS, DRAW
THE POSTMOLD PATTERN ON
THE NOTEBOOK PAPER.

THE PATTERN

<u>STEP 5.</u> EXCAVATE LAYER 3, SIFT AND PLACE THE BEADS IN A PAPER
BAG MARKED "LAYER 3." YOU WILL STILL BE ABLE
TO SEE THE 12 BLACK CIRCLES. THEN EXCAVATE LAYER
4 IN THE SAME MANNER. PUT THE BEADS IN A PAPER
BAG MARKED "LAYER 4." REMEMBER YOUR FIELD NOTES!

<u>STEP 6.</u> EXCAVATE THE NEXT LAYER AND PUT THE BEADS IN THE
PAPER BAG MARKED "LAYER 5." NOTICE THAT THE 12
BLACK CIRCLES ARE GONE. HAD THESE BEEN REAL POST-
MOLDS, YOU WOULD HAVE DESTROYED AN ARCHAEOLO-
GICAL RECORD THAT HAD LAIN IN THE SOIL FOR OVER
1000 YEARS. IF YOU HAD NOT <u>RECORDED</u> AND <u>REPORTED</u>
THIS INFORMATION, IT WOULD HAVE BEEN LOST FOREVER.

<u>STEP 7.</u> EXCAVATE THE BOTTOM LAYER. SIFT THE SAND AS
BEFORE. NOTE THAT THERE ARE NO BEADS IN LAYER
6. ENTER THIS IN YOUR FIELD NOTES.

INTERPRETING THE STRATIGRAPHY FROM YOUR NOTES, MAP, AND PROFILE

LAY OUT THE BEADS FROM EACH LAYER.
ARE ALL THE BEADS FROM A GIVEN LAYER
OF THE SAME COLOR? THERE MAY BE A
FEW THAT ARE OUT OF PLACE. THIS WILL
SHOW YOU HOW DIFFICULT IT IS FOR THE
ARCHAEOLOGIST, WHEN EXCAVATING A
REAL SITE, TO AVOID MIXING ARTIFACTS
FROM DIFFERENT LAYERS. ALSO, THE LAYERS ON A REAL
SITE ARE SELDOM AS CLEARLY VISIBLE AS THE ONES IN
THIS BOX. PRETEND THAT EACH COLOR OF BEADS REPRESENTS
ARTIFACTS FROM A DIFFERENT CULTURAL PERIOD. FROM THE
STRATIGRAPHY IN THE BOX, WHICH COLOR OF SAND AND BEADS
WOULD REPRESENT THE HISTORIC PERIOD?
WHICH THE MISSISSIPPIAN PERIOD?
WHICH THE WOODLAND PERIOD?
WHICH THE ARCHAIC PERIOD?
AND WHICH THE PALEO INDIAN PERIOD?

THE DARK CIRCLES REPRESENT A POSTMOLD PATTERN, REMAINS
OF A HOUSE. FROM YOUR MAP, CAN YOU TELL THE SHAPE OF
THIS HOUSE? IN WHICH CULTURAL PERIOD WAS THE HOUSE BUILT?
HOW DO YOU KNOW FOR SURE THAT IT COULD ONLY HAVE BEEN
BUILT DURING THAT PERIOD? WHAT CAN YOU SAY ABOUT LAYER 6?

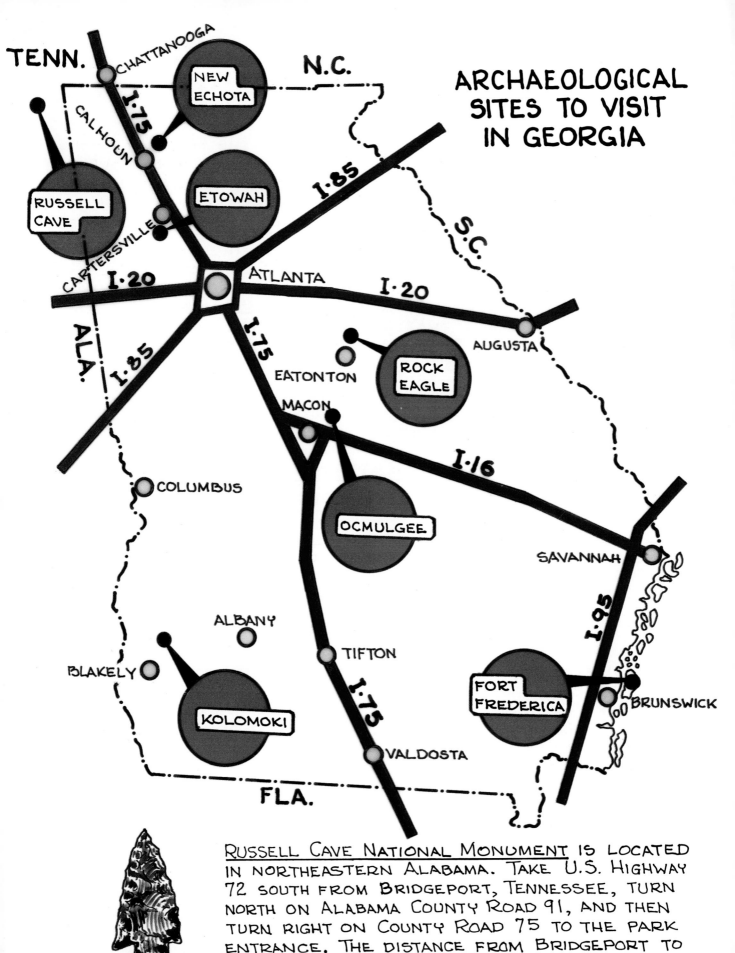

ARCHAEOLOGICAL SITES TO VISIT IN GEORGIA

TENN.

N.C.

CHATTANOOGA

NEW ECHOTA

I·75

CALHOUN

S.C.

RUSSELL CAVE

ETOWAH

I·85

CARTERSVILLE

I·20

ATLANTA

I·20

AUGUSTA

ALA.

I·85

I·75

EATONTON

ROCK EAGLE

MACON

I·16

COLUMBUS

OCMULGEE

SAVANNAH

I·95

ALBANY

TIFTON

BLAKELY

FORT FREDERICA

BRUNSWICK

KOLOMOKI

I·75

VALDOSTA

FLA.

RUSSELL CAVE NATIONAL MONUMENT IS LOCATED IN NORTHEASTERN ALABAMA. TAKE U.S. HIGHWAY 72 SOUTH FROM BRIDGEPORT, TENNESSEE, TURN NORTH ON ALABAMA COUNTY ROAD 91, AND THEN TURN RIGHT ON COUNTY ROAD 75 TO THE PARK ENTRANCE. THE DISTANCE FROM BRIDGEPORT TO THE PARK IS 8 MILES. THE PARK HAS A MUSEUM

AND DEMONSTRATIONS OF PREHISTORIC STONE WORKING. THE CAVE WAS OCCUPIED AS EARLY AS 7,000 B.C.

NEW ECHOTA STATE HISTORIC SITE IS LOCATED 3 MILES EAST OF I-75 ON GEORGIA HIGHWAY 225. IT HAS A MUSEUM AND SEVERAL RECONSTRUCTED INDIAN BUILDINGS. YOU WILL VISIT A PRINT SHOP WHERE THE INDIANS PUBLISHED THEIR OWN NEWSPAPER. NEW ECHOTA WAS THE CHEROKEE CAPITOL FROM 1825 TO 1838.

KOLOMOKI MOUNDS STATE PARK THIS STATE PARK IS 6 MILES NORTH OF BLAKELY, JUST OFF GEORGIA HIGHWAY 27. IT HAS A SMALL MUSEUM AND AN IN SITU BURIAL EXHIBIT. THERE ARE SEVERAL LARGE MOUNDS THAT WERE USED AS PLATFORMS AND FOR BURIAL PURPOSES. KOLOMOKI WAS AN IMPORTANT CEREMONIAL CENTER OF THE WOODLAND AND MISSIS- SIPPIAN PERIODS.

ROCK EAGLE MOUND BELONGS TO THE 4-H CLUBS OF GEORGIA. IT IS LOCATED 7 MILES NORTH OF EATONTON ON U.S. HIGHWAY 129-441. THIS STONE MOUND, IN THE SHAPE OF AN EAGLE, CAN BE VIEWED FROM A TOWER. ROCK EAGLE WAS A CEREMONIAL CENTER OF THE WOODLAND PERIOD.

OCMULGEE NATIONAL MONUMENT IS LOCATED ON U.S. HIGHWAY 80 ON THE OUTSKIRTS OF MACON. THE PARK HAS A LARGE MUSEUM, SEVERAL LARGE TEMPLE MOUNDS, AND A RECONSTRUCTED EARTHLODGE. THIS EARTHLODGE IS THE HIGH- LIGHT OF YOUR VISIT TO OCMULGEE. TOURS AND DEMONSTRATIONS ARE SOMETIMES CONDUCTED BY CREEK INDIANS. OCMULGEE WAS OCCUPIED FROM PALEO INDIAN TIMES TO THE HISTORIC PERIOD.

ETOWAH MOUNDS ARCHAEOLOGICAL AREA IS A STATE PARK LOCATED 5 MILES WEST OF I-75 NEAR CARTERSVILLE. IT HAS A FINE MUSEUM WITH MANY ARTIFACTS AND EXHIBITS. THE MOUNDS ARE SPECTACULAR. ETOWAH WAS AN IMPORTANT CEREMONIAL CENTER DURING THE MISSISSIPPIAN PERIOD.

FORT FREDERICA NATIONAL MONUMENT THIS FORT, LOCATED ON ST. SIMONS ISLAND ACROSS FROM BRUNSWICK, WAS BUILT AS THE MAJOR DEFENSE OF THE NEW COLONY OF GEORGIA BY GEN. JAMES OGLETHORPE IN 1736.

WHY IS ARCHAEOLOGY IMPORTANT?

As you have seen, archaeology tells us the story of human culture in the past. This is an important story, because it shows us how we have come to be the way we are in the modern world. By reconstructing this story, we can enrich our present lives, and we can plan better for the future.

Thus far, archaeologists have written a story of 12,000 years of human development in Georgia. We have followed this story from the Paleo Indians to the Archaic and Woodland people, to the Mississippians, and finally to the historic cultures of Indians, Blacks and Whites. However, the story is incomplete.

Every summer, archaeologists and their students, from one or more universities, take to the field in Georgia to explore some of our past. Sometimes they study very ancient prehistoric sites. Other times they excavate sites of our recent history. Wherever culture is buried, whether it be in fields, woods, or under city streets, archaeology can add to our knowledge of ourselves. There are still many frontiers in the soil!

ALWAYS REMEMBER, ARCHAEOLOGICAL SITES ARE AN "ENDANGERED SPECIES." ONCE THEY ARE DESTROYED, THEY ARE DESTROYED FOREVER, AND THE INFORMATION THEY CONTAIN IS DESTROYED FOREVER. ONLY TRAINED ARCHAEOLOGISTS SHOULD DIG IN SITES. HELP ARCHAEOLOGISTS PRESERVE THE PAST. IT BELONGS TO ALL OF US!